D0897203

HAPPY ARE YOU POOR

THOMAS DUBAY, S.M.

HAPPY ARE YOU POOR

The Simple Life
and
Spiritual Freedom

IGNATIUS PRESS   SAN FRANCISCO

Original edition published by Dimension Books, Denville, N.J.
© 1981 by Thomas Dubay, S.M.
Published with ecclesiastical approval
Reprinted by permission

Cover art: *The Angelus*, by Jean Francois Millet (1814–1875)
Musée d'Orsay, Paris, France
Cover design by Riz Boncan Marsella

Second edition © 2003 by Thomas Dubay, S.M.
All rights reserved
Published by Ignatius Press, San Francisco
ISBN 0-89870-921-0
Library of Congress Control Number 2002105232
Printed in the United States of America ∞

CONTENTS

PREFACE

Books should not be written unless they are needed. Given the bell curve phenomenon in the distribution of human abilities, it is not surprising that most writings, religious or secular, do not rise above the level of mediocrity. Many merely repeat what has been far better said elsewhere. Some are merely trivial even if superbly crafted. Others create interest for no better reason than that they shock some and attract others by revolting against society's sensibilities or the Church's teaching.

It ill becomes an author to express a confident judgment regarding the merit of his work. If he is sensitive, he is acutely aware of its limitations, and he wishes someone would do a far better job with the same material. But if a book is needed, he sits down and does what he can.

This volume is, in my judgment, needed. In recent years a few worthwhile works on poverty have appeared, but this present one does not repeat their messages, and it does not follow their approaches. The table of contents indicates fairly well what these pages do attempt.

Happy Are You Poor is addressed to everyone in all vocations of life. It seeks to meet the readers where they are (good intentions in this question of material goods but often with much confusion) and to bring them to where they would like to be (completely possessed by God and not by things).

I wish to express gratitude to the editor of *Pastoral Life* for graciously allowing me to use in Chapter 14 sections of two of my articles which have appeared in that periodical.

This volume is dedicated to the Mother of him who became poor for our sakes (2 Cor 8:9). She saw his poverty firsthand, and she lived it with him. He gave in turn to her as to no other to rejoice in God her Savior.

PART I

PROBLEMS AND PRESUPPOSITIONS

I

Universal Radicality

To the unprepared eyes of modern men and women the title of this book can hardly be taken seriously. To suggest that poverty is desirable seems to approach absurdity. To imply that it is somehow meant for all people in every vocation may seem outrageous. Yet you have picked up this volume and begun to read. Could it be that some small voice is urging this outrage upon you?

Could it be that this book is written for you?

When most people think of poverty, they think of destitution. They envision squalor, malnutrition, ragged clothing, dire housing, omnipresent dirt, the absence of necessities for a decent human life. Whatever gospel poverty might mean, they do not take seriously the thought that destitution is a viable option for themselves.

When they who are better educated in the faith dwell on the idea of Gospel poverty, knowing that it does not mean destitution, they turn their thoughts in the direction of religious life. They have heard of a vow of poverty, and, feeling no call to a vowed life, they dismiss the thought of it quite as readily as the thought of destitution. Obviously a married person cannot seriously entertain either choice as compatible with the roles of responsible spouse and parent.

Yet this same person committed to Christ is probably aware that the Gospel repeatedly speaks of an ideal of poverty, and he wonders whether any of these many references are meant for him. In the liturgy throughout the year, weekdays and Sundays alike, one hears over and over again that the poor are blessed, that we must renounce all that we possess to be a disciple of Christ, that if a person has two tunics and a needy brother has none he must give one away, that it is easier for a camel to pass through the eye of a needle than for a rich man to enter heaven, that we came into the world with nothing and shall leave it with nothing and therefore we ought to be content with food and clothing and gladly give up superfluities. These things are routinely read to all the faithful, these and much else in the same vein.

All this is stark. Admittedly. Indeed, for one who takes the Gospel seriously, it is frightening. Could it possibly be meant for such as the likes of me?

To put the question differently: Is a book which professes to deal with a radical frugality meant only for the person who has a vocation to monastery or convent? Could it be directed also to the laity, even if in somewhat different manners and nuances of meaning? And if it is meant for laymen, would they not be eccentrics on the fringes of society? Almost no normal married person thinks of poverty as an ideal or even a possible way to raise a family. Are there, then, really two Gospel messages about the use of material things? Or is there basically only one?

Perplexity at this point is understandable. Our very next chapter will spell out the confusion in considerable detail, and following chapters will hopefully unravel the obscurities and problems and mysteries. Unfortunately almost nothing is said from our pulpits that would present the faithful with a clear, systematic understanding of the New Testament doctrine on our use of material goods.

Our original question remains: Is this book meant for you? If you are a cleric or religious, the answer obviously is yes. If you are a layman, the answer is again yes—even if it is not obvious to you at the moment. I must say that the answer is emphatically yes.

Scripture scholars seem to be of one mind (I have come across no one of another mind) that most New Testament texts that deal with poverty as an ideal are meant to be applied to all who follow Christ. Some commentators go so far as to say that all such texts are said of everyone without exception. These latter writers are mistaken in their sweeping universality, for there are some texts that are directed to a comparatively small group who are invited to give up their very property for the kingdom. But with the exception of these few texts, all the rest are meant for all classes and all states in life. No doubt all this requires a full justification and explanation. Such will be offered in the pages that follow.

Whom, then, does this work envision? First, the laity. There are many persons, young, middle aged, and elderly, who are yearning for the undiluted message of Christ. They do not want it to be exaggerated, and yet they seek the radical word and wish to live it in their lives. The fact that virginity offers a unique type of freedom for a thoroughgoing pursuit of the kingdom does not imply that laymen are called to an inferior holiness. The greatest of all commandments, that we love God with our whole heart, whole soul, and whole mind, is by definition a totality commandment, and it is directed to all classes of people without exception. States in life vary in the efficiency with which they lead to the goal, but the goal remains the same for all. The laymen's living of frugality must differ in some ways from that of the religious and cleric. But the difference is not that between mediocrity and excellence. Evangelical poverty is radical, and it is radical for all.

That the message of this volume is meant for laymen will become progressively more clear as we proceed in our discussion. This clarity especially stands out in Chapters 5 and 9, when we explain why evangelical poverty is so beautiful and freeing an ideal. Because it is a negation in itself, poverty is not sought for its own sake but for what it makes possible and much easier to attain: a radical readiness, a sensitivity to what Jesus is about, a sharing with the needy, an apostolic credibility, a pilgrim witness in a world of dwindling resources. These are values, precious values, to our laity as well as to clergy and religious.

Though these pages are directed to all ages, classes, and stations in life, they may have a special appeal to youth. Many of our best young people, enjoying as they do the natural idealism of their years, see with some keenness (though, if they continue to grow, they will see far better later on) the superficiality and shallowness and emptiness of a pursuit of material things for their own sakes. I notice in religious congregations that often the young members as a group offer less resistance to the radicality of gospel poverty than do the middle aged as a group. This by no means suggests that we lack young people who are clothes conscious, car loving, pleasure seeking. Nor are we implying that we lack middle-aged men and women who want to be poor with the poor Christ. What I am suggesting is that even though some of our youth do not live up to their nonmaterialistic ideals, they often seem more open to persuasion than many of their elders.

It goes without saying that this work is also directed to those who have embraced the evangelical counsels in religious life. What is said for everyone of course applies to them. Yet because their commitment to Gospel poverty includes some elements proper to their life, Chapter 13 is devoted to their situation. They have read and heard all sorts of conflicting views as to what their vow means and does not mean. One who works much with religious knows how widespread and various are the confusions that bedevil serious men and women who wish to give all to the Master. Hopefully this volume will aid them in clarifying their thoughts and strengthening their resolves.

Finally, we envision bishops and priests, diocesan as well as religious. If the frugality values mentioned above are to be lived by laypersons, by the sheep of the Lord's flock, they surely are to be lived by the shepherds. Peter, the first shepherd, tells other leaders in the first-century Church that they are to be a pattern the flock can follow (1 Pet 5:3). Priests and bishops should know Gospel poverty well, for they are to proclaim it to the faithful—it is part of the deposit committed to their care and pastoral solicitude. But they are first to live what they proclaim (Mt 5:16, 19). Because they enjoy a special configuration to Christ the High Priest through the sacrament of orders, a special chapter will be devoted to their reliving of his poverty.

This book is not difficult to grasp, but it does require thinking. Pat solutions to complex problems may appeal to superficial minds, but they have no staying power in any mind. The vague generalizations and flowery jargon that have characterized not a little of recent writing on the subject of evangelical poverty have usually veiled a shallowness of understanding, if not a positive dilution of meaning. Too often the effort to bridge the sizable gap between the radical Gospel message and our lukewarm Christian practice has yielded not much more than a vapid void. Sound theology is deep, interwoven, of one piece. Dislodging one piece involves dislodging the whole. Misplacing one bolt in a complex jet engine destroys the whole mechanism. John Henry Newman once explained that his conversion to the Church could not be expressed in a short formula:

"Catholicism is a deep matter—you cannot take it up in a tea-cup." To understand his reasons for becoming a Catholic he insisted that "you must consent to *think*".[1] So it is with gospel poverty: one must consent to think.

---

1. Wilfrid Ward, *The Life of John Henry Newman*, vol. 1, pp. 121, 122; the emphasis is Newman's.

2

Are You Confused?

This book is radical. It is not in the least exaggerated, however. Its contents are simple enough for a schoolboy to grasp, and yet most adults go to their graves without a real feel for it. The message is austere, but at the same time it bears tidings of great joy.

Perhaps we ought not to be surprised that on this subject of Gospel poverty confusion reigns even among sincere people. Although the New Testament, which we hear read in our liturgies, speaks of it dozens of times, most people in all vocations of life would admit they are not at all sure just what they should think and do about the matter. Reading books and articles may aggravate rather than remedy the uncertainty, for one finds in them a welter of opinions, opinions often in conflict with one another. One could without cynicism ask, if all this is true, why should he pick up this book and hope to do better. Though the author is personally convinced that there are ways to come through the thicket of confusion, he will leave it to the reader's judgment to determine whether he has succeeded in pointing them out.

However, I should like to begin by facing head-on the confusion itself. What are our problems, our hesitations, our doubts regarding the subject of this book? I can easily think of thirty or forty questions that have been raised in recent years. At this point we shall merely notice the problems.

Through the course of the following chapters we shall propose pointers to their solutions.

Concepts of Gospel Poverty

Our first group of questions deals with the very nature of the poverty lived and taught by Jesus. When we speak of the evangelical ideal, what exactly are we talking about? In the literature of our day all sorts of proposals have been offered as to what this poverty means or ought to mean. We may present these proposals in the form of questions.

Is the poverty envisioned in this study the same thing as destitution? When Jesus requires that his disciples give up everything they possess (Lk 14:33), is he demanding that we embrace the dire despair of those who experience aching stomachs, ragged clothing, shanty dwellings, proneness to illness, and premature death?

Or is the Gospel ideal merely a spirit of poverty, an inner detachment, a readiness to be separated from material things when love of neighbor or circumstances of life require it? Can a married couple or a religious community enjoying a beautiful, well-furnished home be content that they are living the Lord's teaching provided that they do not cling to these goods and are willing to give them up should duty require it?

May poverty be translated simply by the word moderation? And when we speak of moderation, would we say that people are moderate when they live on the level of their brothers and sisters, having neither a great deal more nor a great deal less? If we answer affirmatively, we then must ask: Who are the brothers and sisters? Are they the people in this block or rural area? Or are they everyone in this city . . . or this state . . . or this nation? Or in our global village, would our neighbors include the third and fourth worlds as well as the first and second? If one answers yes to this last question, how could he possibly get norms for poverty when there are such vast differences among the four worlds?

Or does the evangelical ideal have little or nothing to do with material things? Is it rather personal relationships, an availability of one's time, person, talents? Could it be that the very knottiness of the questions we have already asked as well as those we shall ask later itself indicates that we ought to rethink the Gospel teaching in completely fresh terms? Could seeing this counsel as availability cut through our tiring efforts to define a material concept? Or would this redefinition simply be a rationalization, an unwillingness to wrestle with Gospel radicality? Is "availability" so vague an ideal that anyone could satisfy himself that he is living it? Is it what the Gospel texts are talking about?

Is economy identical with evangelical poverty? Is one being poor when he watches assiduously for sales, when he buys inferior goods that will wear out soon even if in the long run he may pay more for them and their early replacements?

Is the evangelical ideal a factual frugality, a sparing use of material things? Whatever its motivation, is it a factual situation? Must one have little in order to be faithful to Jesus' example and teaching?

Or is the Lord's message essentially a sharing of material goods with one's neighbor, so that one is living the Lord's word no matter how much he may own provided he is using it for the good of others and not merely to satisfy his own desires for pleasure and comfort?

Does poverty imply a lack of security? Do owning one's home, possessing a permanent job, having stocks and investments show a lack of trust in divine providence? If one responds affirmatively to this last question, could he claim to be imitating the Master, who had no place to lay his head? If one answers negatively, must he be committed to saying that large numbers of the faithful both lay and religious are not living the Gospel?

Since security (as most people envision it) is closely allied with power, worldly power, would the Gospel require that we give up this power? An education to the level of a doctoral degree gives one no little capacity for acquiring wealth and comfort and pleasure. Is there an intrinsic contradiction between poverty and power? And would we not have to add to academic power other types such as those associated with excelling competence in athletics, acting ability, music? Can one be highly gifted and poor at the same time?

Lastly, is Gospel poverty mostly a sign or a witness, so that what is primary is not the factual situation but rather what appears, what one's lifestyle says to others? If the answer is yes, how does this definition really differ from factual frugality? Could one actually separate clear witness from living in a sparing manner? Is a sham sign a sign?

Theoretical Problems

If the reader is not already discouraged or dismayed beyond repair, we may proceed to still further questions. Among them we may ask first of all whether the meaning of Gospel poverty has changed in recent years. Indeed, is this meaning susceptible to change, or is it some sort of immutable value? There is no doubt that many religious have spoken about redefining the three vows they take. They at least feel that poverty has no immutable essence determined once and for all. If its nature may change with time, who is to say what the new meaning is? May each person determine it for himself? May private individuals change the meaning of revelation?—for an evangelical counsel is by definition a part of the revelation given in and through Christ.

If creation is good and given for our use, why should it be given up? Supposing we take a positive view of the universe and all that is in it, can one rightly say that denying a use of things is objectively better than enjoyment and security and wealth? And if somehow doing without things is an ideal to be pursued, how do we fit the ideal to a state in life, marriage, that is itself by definition concerned with this world? Supposing further that the ideal can be fitted with marriage, would there not be more differences than likenesses between its practice there and in religious life?

What connection does the freely chosen poverty of Sacred Scripture have with the unfreely suffered deprivations of the billions in the third and fourth worlds? International economic systems and practices are so immensely complex that most of us would not claim to understand them completely. We are hardly in a position to evaluate the heated pros and cons directed at capitalism and the sundry types of socialism. Nor are many of us acquainted with liberation theology, responsible or irresponsible. Furthermore, even if we grant that we in the have nations should share our wealth with the have-not nations in whatever ways that may be possible, those who believe in the Gospel could at best remedy only a fraction of the huge needs around our globe. How does all this relate to the biblical sparing-sharing use of material goods?

If factual frugality embraced in faith is the lofty ideal we shall see it to be, why do so terribly few followers of Christ embrace it in a serious manner? Is the ideal real for fallen human nature? Even they who take a vow of evangelical poverty are seldom radical in living the vow. Few people in our society are inclined to look upon religious as particularly noteworthy in living a sparing-sharing way of life. No doubt there are exceptions: vowed men and women scattered in the established communities and in newly founded radical ones. These few are poor with the poor Christ. Happily refreshing as they are, we all know only too well the many examples of vowed men and women who dine and drink on an upper-middle-class level; who possess extensive wardrobes, who enjoy expensive recreations, vacations, pleasure trips; who in the evenings and on weekends seldom are home enjoying the simple, deep things of life.

And what of the laity? They too are called to the heights of holiness. If Scripture scholars are correct in their contention that most by far of Gospel texts on Christic poverty are meant for all classes in the Church, would we not expect that generous married men and women (and of course the single layperson) would also be outstanding for their sparing lifestyles? After all, do we not read that they who can but do not share material goods with needy brothers and sisters have a dead faith (Jas 2:14–17)? Are we not bluntly told that one, anyone, cannot love God who does not share his good things with the deprived neighbor (1 Jn 3:17–18)? It was laymen who asked what they had to do to prove their conversion of heart, and it was they who heard from fiery John the Baptist: if you have two tunics and your brother has none, give him one; and do the same with food (Lk 3:10–11). Faith, love, conversion: the heart of holiness. They are impossible without the sharing of material possessions. Yet how many laymen really shine as stars in the midst of a perverse generation (Phil 2:15)?

And what of the clergy? If the previous paragraph must be addressed to the flock, it must first be addressed to the leaders of the flock. Else they would be in the position of speaking but not doing. It goes without saying that the message of this volume should be proclaimed frequently from our Sunday and weekday pulpits. The poverty ideal appears over and over again in the pages of the New Testament. Yes, and the Old too. Yahweh's wrath rages against priests who have forgotten the teaching of their God and fail to proclaim it (see Hos 4:4–6; Jer 23:1–2; Ezek 34 *in toto*). The pastoral letters to leaders insist that the undiluted message is to be proclaimed in season and out of season, welcome or unwelcome (2 Tim 4:1–5). These same apostolic men are to avoid superfluities, for they, like all of us, came into the world with nothing and will leave it with nothing (1 Tim 6:7–8). They are to live the message and then proclaim it. Such is the ideal. Our immediate question is the reality of the practice. Once again, there are exemplary bishops and diocesan priests, some of whom live on the borders of destitution, and that of their free choice. But no one would claim that such is the general pattern. In this sense is evangelical poverty real?

Practical Questions

If most of the New Testament sayings about frugality are directed to all persons, how do husbands and wives possibly live this radicality and yet provide for themselves and their children? Secular society is hardly imbued with Gospel principles, and so married people cannot count on others to care for their children and for their own old age. And even in an evangelical community there is the pauline admonition that they who do not work do not eat (2 Thess 3:10; cf. also 3:7–9). It is well and good to preach the sparing-sharing ideal, but how do sincere people much in love with God live that ideal in the nitty gritty of a hardnosed world?

Most of us live in community: marriage, religious life, rectory. A community incarnates itself in many ways, one of them being its shared material goods. Is it important that the members of the group be of one mind as to the meaning and the practical bearing of Gospel frugality? Is it possible for an individual to live this message in a thoroughgoing way if he lacks the support and, in a way, the "permission" of the other members? There is no doubt that the individual can live many aspects of a radically simple way of life even if others do not, but it remains true that he will meet not a few problems in his day-by-day efforts. If communal support is important, how is it achieved?

This last question suggests still another: How can change be brought about? An immense immobility characterizes this whole problem of getting members of an affluent society even to discuss voluntary poverty in a manner that leads to practice. Books and articles have poured off our presses since the 1960s. Lectures and conferences and committee meetings and position papers have been multiplied almost beyond measure. Yet little happens in actual life. We have had a Niagara of words, a trickle of action. Given this enormous immobility, how do we explain it? How can any effective change be brought about?

Once again this last question prompts another: Can personal or communal poverty be legislated? Could the Church feasibly publish, if not laws, at least persuading norms? Should she go further than Vatican Council II did in urging priests and bishops to voluntary poverty and require some concrete steps toward factual frugality? Should religious institutes (which were told explicitly to be poor both in fact and in spirit)[1] legislate details of a factually poor way of life according to the charisms and aims of each order? Most likely many

---

[1] Vatican II, *Perfectae caritatis*, Decree on the Up-to-date Renewal of Religious Life (October 28, 1965), no. 13.

laypersons, priests, and religious would have rapid-fire answers to these questions. How valid would these rapid answers be?

With the three or four dozen questions this chapter has raised, the reader may well be on the verge of a practical scepticism. If there are differing views on all these problems, how can we possibly come to sound conclusions? Yet Jesus prayed that his community be "completely one" (Jn 17:23), and Saint Paul insisted that the faithful be "in perfect agreement", of a common voice and one mind (Rom 15:6; Phil 2:1–2). If a sparing-sharing lifestyle is connected with love for God and a living faith, with a conversion of life, we may not disagree. Being completely one must include at rock bottom the essentials of the Gospel. Sharing with the needy brother and sister is one of the essentials.

Despite the magnitude of the problem of disagreement, it must, with divine help, be possible to achieve unity of mind. We cannot be commanded to achieve the impossible. What then would the criteria be according to which a sincere community may think rightly about a faith-inspired frugality?

3

Becoming Unconfused:
Criteria for Solution

Although at this point in our discussion finding clear answers may seem hopeless, such is not the case. But before indicating why, I may add still another difficulty that is a fact, not merely a question. In matters that touch on one's style of life, most people have a heavy emotional and volitional investment. They find it difficult, indeed almost impossible, to investigate the evidence coolly and calmly. One of the easiest ways to elicit a strong response from an individual in conversation or from an audience in a lecture is to make a telling point or two that even mildly suggests that they are self-indulgent in their use of money. Prayerful people tend to welcome any admonition that shows them that their way of life does not measure up to the Gospel, but others easily get indignant and sometimes angry. And of course one who is subject to indignation or anger is not likely to think clearly, nor is he sensitive to evidence that runs counter to his manner of life. For that reason the present chapter will have to be followed by one on premises, on the conditions necessary for understanding evangelical poverty (indeed, evangelical anything).

Rising from a Rootless Relativism

Our first step toward clarifying our maze of problems is to recognize that not all answers are of equal value. To some people this is entirely obvious; to others it is not. Many today will respond to conflicting theories of evangelical poverty by remarking that "your position is suitable for you and mine is suitable for me. God reads our hearts; he does not ask that we be scholars. You go your way, and I will go mine."

My first comment on this view is that it is light years removed from the attitudes of Jesus and Saint Paul and the rest of the New Testament writers. While there is room for some differences in concrete applications, the Gospel doctrine is clear and specific. And, especially to the point here, it does not permit contradictory diversity. This remark calls for a distinction. A complementary diversity can be good, for in this case different people may be offering insights that complete and enrich one another. They may all be correct. A contradictory diversity is damaging; it can be a disaster. Why? The logician points out that in a contradiction (in which one affirms and another denies exactly what has been affirmed and in the same sense) there is no mutual enrichment. One must be right, and one must be wrong. Which is to say that one must be out of touch with reality. If the reality is important, the result of being out of touch can be a catastrophe. Contradictory opinions, therefore, about social justice, evangelical poverty, sexual morality, and so on are not all equally valid. To hold otherwise is to hold a rootless relativism. It is to be either non- or anti-intellectual, for one operates not on the basis of objective evidences but on no basis at all other than one's desires and emotions and will.

Why Do People Differ?

To ask the question of why people disagree in contradictory manners is implicitly to ask why some are right and some are wrong. To analyze this problem fully would itself require a book, but happily our purposes can be met by a sketchy account of key ideas. The first of these keys lies in the area of concepts and definitions. Though they may use the same words, people often disagree because they are using them in different senses or because their definitions are ill conceived or ill expressed. If five people have five divergent concepts of evangelical poverty, it can be no surprise that they must begin by carefully thought out and expressed definitions. Adequate definitions will make it clear whether their differences are complementary (and therefore mutually enriching) or contradictory (and therefore damaging to one side at least). If one has engaged much in discussions of Gospel poverty, he will agree that only too often people express their opinions without defining their terms.

Our second key reason to explain varying opinions is that the "facts" presented in the discussion are not facts. Political life abounds in examples of individuals vehemently expressing their opinions about international relations or energy problems or labor-management conflicts and yet being quite uninformed about the complex factual data involved. If one has not studied with some thoroughness the biblical revelation dealing with material goods together with the early patristic literature, the medieval theologians, and contemporary thinkers, he may be more than a little mistaken as to what he conceives the facts of the matter to be. Understandably he is likely to disagree with someone who has so studied the matter.

The third key is perhaps least understood of all, and yet it is the most pervasive and difficult to correct. Few people even suspect that it is operative in their lives, and even fewer give it any prolonged attention. People are mistaken, especially in ultimate matters, because their fundamental presuppositions and principles are incorrect, unreal. Our most radical views and positions are so deeply a part of us that it is a rare person who gives much thought to them. Yet they profoundly affect and color our opinions and decisions. We "read" facts and evidences through the lenses of our basic principles, and so individuals with radically different basic principles look at the same data and come up with opposite conclusions. For example, if a man holds that there is no knowledge but sense knowledge, and if he is consistent with this presupposition (which of course he cannot prove), he must reject all sorts of evidences for extrasensory perception, for creation in time, for miracles, for the soul, for religion. No matter what evidences are produced, he will interpret them through his presupposition. Likewise, if a person holds that prestige is a major value in human life, he is constantly going to disagree with another who holds that humility is a major value. Each of them reads human situations according to his fundamental premise. So also the theist and the non-theist will logically disagree with each other about the ideas in this volume. It cannot be otherwise.

We therefore have some initial suggestions for the solution of our many problems regarding Gospel poverty. The first suggestion responds to our first key: thorough study and research. Scripture itself tells us, "Before you speak, learn" (Sir 18:19, RSV). Not everyone of course can be a scholar; lack of time and/or talent prevents it. But the conclusion we draw is not that no one may speak, but rather that one should not assert a position unless he knows from an unerring teacher or he has mastered the subject for himself. The next suggestion responds to the last key: attaining ultimate truth requires conversion of mind and heart. People imbibe correct and valid basic principles when they honestly and selflessly pursue absolute truth, goodness, beauty. God gives light to the humble, the pure, the loving. And we are not such until we are converted from the distortions flowing from our original fall and our personal sins. A serious attempt to live a God-centered life is an indispensable condition for doing theology—and indeed for understanding evangelical poverty in the context of the Christic economy. This is one reason the saints are so important later on in this study: they are converted, wonderfully converted, heroically converted.

Primary Criteria

Supposing then that we are careful in defining our terms, assiduous in our study of relevant sources, and converted at least in the sense that God is our consuming desire and love, we ask next what the norms may be that will guide us to valid answers to the many questions asked in Chapter 2. Norms there must be, of course. Otherwise we flounder in emotionalism and/or voluntarism, both of which are forms of anti-intellectualism.

It is well for us to note, indeed to emphasize, that everyone has basic premises from which he draws his practical conclusions. Hence, if one should disagree with what we say further on about practicalities, it is most likely that his premises differ from the ones we present in this chapter. He may not be aware of his premises, but there is no doubt that he has them. As I write these pages I, too, have fundamental premises and I wish to face them, to make them clear to the reader. What is proposed further on in this volume is based on these root criteria. What they are we now consider.

1 *New Testament revelation.* The meaning of evangelical poverty is learned from the lips of the Lord, or it is not learned at all. We are not dealing with a mere humanism, nor are we engaged in a sociological study. We are looking into a divinely revealed plan for the equitable use of material goods in this world. We intend that they lead us and our brothers and sisters to the bosom of trinitarian life in our final fulfillment.

2 *The teaching Church.* Jesus did not commit his message to private persons but to a community, the *ekklesia.* They who listen to his representatives listen to him; they who reject these representatives reject him (Lk 10:16). Together with the rest of Christic revelation, his teaching about poverty has been committed to the care and proclamation of this Church. Just as a nation's fundamental constitution needs to be interpreted by a living judicial system, so our fundamental Gospel documents must be authoritatively interpreted by a living teacher. Happily this living teacher enjoys a divinely originated authenticity that merely human judicial systems do not. Hence the Church's understanding of evangelical poverty is crucial for any who would be a brother of the Lord: "He who hears you, hears me."

3 *Consistency with the rest of revelation.* The divine disclosure is a closely knit whole. One doctrine cannot be rejected without that rejection affecting other doctrines. It is both interesting and significant that they who reject a single teaching usually go on eventually to reject others and, sometimes, the whole. It is doubly significant that they never succeed in presenting to their listeners or readers a substitute and consistent whole to replace what they have mutilated. Each of the interlinking parts of our theology strengthens the others, and each multiplies the probative power of the others. In his

Essay on Development Newman noted that a person may easily object to one doctrine by itself and seem to have something of a case when the related doctrines are not considered (and this is common in merely popular articles and conversations), but for any thinking, informed person this objecter is demolished by the weight of the whole. And so it is with our doctrine on poverty. It is tightly interwoven with the primacy of God, with humility and fraternal love, with self-denial and the paschal mystery, with apostolic freedom and consecrated virginity, with a radical readiness for the kingdom that all, married and nonmarried alike, must possess. Any valid teaching on the use of material goods will fit coherently with the entire Gospel message.

4 *"From their fruits you will know them."* This criterion is itself revealed. The authenticity or inauthenticity of a given concept of poverty can be seen from the consequences that follow in those who live according to it. For example, if one says that Gospel poverty does not imply a sparing-sharing use of material goods but rather refers to our being available to others, the usual consequences show clearly enough that the concept is merely a rationalization, a cover for living a comfortable life. People living elegantly can easily persuade themselves that they are available to others. Furthermore, their definition leads to a diminution of credibility in apostolate. And it does not bring about the inner detachment which is a condition of being a disciple of Jesus (Lk 14:33). It fires no one to undertake heroic enterprises for the kingdom. It implies little or no leadership in sharing with the destitute of the world. From its fruits we know it to be empty of real significance as an evangelical counsel.

5 *The saints.* Our final criterion for knowing what the Gospel does and does not mean is the pattern provided by those

who not only live the revealed message faithfully but who live it heroically. The Church in her liturgy and in her canonizations presents the saints to us for imitation precisely because she finds them authentic witnesses to what the Gospel means and what she herself teaches.

The saints actually are the best examples we have of biblical exegesis. Scripture scholars would be the first to acknowledge that they not rarely contradict one another in their explanations of the sacred word. We have noted that in a genuine contradiction one party must be wrong—which of course means that one must be out of touch with the reality at issue. The saints, however, do not contradict one another in their living of evangelical values. Each is a unique person and has his or her own traits, often charming traits, but when it comes to revealed doctrines and virtues the saints are entirely of one mind. If we wonder, for example, what becoming a little child for the kingdom might mean, we look to Thérèse of Lisieux. But saints in very different external circumstances lived the same doctrine. If we wonder whether publicly taught dissent from clear magisterial teachings is a value, we find no example of it in any of the saints. On the contrary, like Teresa of Avila, they are ready to die for the least of these teachings. So also when it comes to evangelical poverty. With no exception the saints lived a sparing-sharing lifestyle. They unanimously exemplified in their lives the doctrine contained in this volume. What they all did (and what some of them wrote) provides error-free standards by which we may come to know how in the concrete details of our lives the Gospel ideals are to be applied to married life, to priestly life, to religious life. The saints bring the Gospel close in time and space and person. A study of their lives dissolves most of the confusions described in our previous chapter.

The reader will notice that all of the primary criteria I have sketched are revelational. That is, they all relate to God's word. No one of them is merely human wisdom—which, Saint Paul advises the Corinthians, is foolishness to God. This must be the case for the simple reason that we are dealing not with humanism but with evangelical reality. Nothing finite is capable of judging the infinite. No human insight, good as it may be in itself, is an adequate judge of the divine. We can evaluate our use of material goods only in the light shed by him who has made both visible creation and us who use that creation.

Secondary Criteria

However, we should not fail to address some attention to a few assisting guides that may aid us in determining what specifically evangelical poverty requires of us in our modern technological society. Because of their secondary and servant character these guides may not of course contradict our primary norms. Wisely understood and applied, they can be of considerable help in our efforts to make the Gospel come alive in the complicated and manifold details of our sundry states and conditions in life.

The first of these subordinate norms is sociological and political description and analysis. Secular research, study, and publications abound in information about economic conditions in the four worlds. This literature deals with international political policies, supranational corporations, problems of production and distribution, ideological and operational economic structures, consumerism and destitution, goals, and means of international cooperation. We live the Gospel in our world, not in another. We live it in our century, not in another. We may not be ignorant of the hard realities of modern economic life or of the dire straits of billions in our global village.

The second of our ancillary guides is philosophical reflection. Although we derive our primary data from divine revelation, we are not therefore exempted from a pondering of principles accessible to human reason. In a later chapter, for example, we shall argue that a loving community tends to incarnate and express its unity and life in material sharing. This in turn is due to the fact that our tangible goods are as extensions of our persons, and if we love our brother and sister as ourselves we wish them to share in these goods just as we do. One can only regret the shallowness with which Gospel ideals are sometimes discussed in popular articles and everyday conversations. Not only are these ideals lost sight of, but one also finds at times little expenditure of energy in hard thinking.

Lived experience is a third aid, but it may be used only if one has a lively sense of its ambiguity. I find it remarkable how well-educated men and women facilely speak of fashioning their lifestyles from their "lived experience". They seem innocent of the implications of what they are saying. As regards evangelical realities, the value of a man's experience is in direct ratio to his sanctity. How a saint experiences silence and solitude is 180 degrees removed from how a sinner or a mediocre individual experiences them. The former enjoys a profound communion with God, whereas the latter are thoroughly bored. How one reacts to factual frugality varies all the way from the avaricious miser, who can scarcely shake the thought of how he may increase his income, to a Francis of Assisi, who sings in free joy as he wends his pilgrim steps along the roads of Italy.

Our final aid is clear and correct language. Flowery generalizations have their poetic place in human life, but they are of little help when it comes to solving concrete problems. They can be a positive nuisance in theology when they are used as evasions and covers. Vague formulations are sometimes proposed as solutions to doctrinal divisions, for it is thought that agreement to a fuzzy formula is thereby unity or reconciliation. It is, of course, quite the contrary. Least common denominator "agreements" merely cover over divisions, because after the agreement each group goes on to interpret it in its own way. The cleavage deepens.

The criteria sketched in this chapter yield a coherent picture of Gospel poverty. It is my intent to find solutions to the many questions I have raised not by weaving essays from private opinions but by a faithful (even if not complicated) study of the New Testament. We shall then be able to test our understanding by the fruits it yields in contemporary life and by the down-to-earth practice of the saints. By this approach we may be confident of separating the wheat from the chaff.

4

Poverty and Premises

Creation is lush. It abounds and overflows. An oak produces not one acorn per year but dozens and dozens of them year after year, even though one each season would seem far more than enough to reproduce the species. A female fish lays not two or three eggs but millions of them. A lily is so magnificent that if there were only one on the planet, we would count ourselves blessed to have it displayed in our national museum. Season after season, tulip fields in Holland and orchid gardens in Singapore are awash with delicate and breathtaking colors. If one galaxy of a million stars would appear to be an overdone extravaganza, what are we to think of billions of galaxies separated by billions of light years and enclosing billions of giant suns in each of them—and next to our sun, an ordinary star, our earth is like a pea next to a basketball? Then there is the microcosm of the subatomic world, as astonishing in its minute mysteries as the macrocosm is in its vast richness.

Yet beyond all this is the human person. Even on a purely natural level there is nothing in creation that approaches the human brain and spirit. "Ten linguists working full time for 10 years to analyze the structure of the English language could not program a computer with the ability for language[1] acquired by an average child in the first 10 or even five years of life."[2] And it scarcely needs to be pointed out that without human brains behind it a computer is absolutely zero.

One could go on and on. Any branch of study abounds in marvels. Surrounding us on all sides, they may serve to underscore one of our poverty problems: Can we rightly give up the splendors of creation? Is it right to be poor when the message of the universe, and therefore presumably of its Author, is wealth? Who are we to be skimpy when he is bountiful? Why limit our use of his handiwork when he places almost no boundaries to what he has made for our admiration and delight? Why be a small, petty, negativistic ascetic when creation itself proclaims the grand, the great, the munificent, the delightful? One may be inclined to give a pat answer to these questions, namely, that the negative and the ascetic are indeed narrow. Self-denial may be seen as well-intentioned but as unhealthy nonetheless.

Not so. There are men and women who cannot, or at least do not, get themselves to think seriously and at some length about Gospel poverty because they choose to consider God as comfortable and pleasant, not awesome and just and meaning exactly what he says. These people choose—it is a choice, not a necessity—to look upon the beauties of nature and the overall "goodness of people" and then to conclude that the "woe to you rich" and "how happy are you poor ones" (Lk 6:24, 20) cannot be taken without major qualifications that strip them of their message. After all, they reason, there are many respectable, honest, rich families in

---

[1] For example, dissecting units of sound and meaning, rules for recombining sounds and words and intricate patterns for taking turns in dialogue.

[2] Breyne Moskowitz, *Scientific American*, Nov. 1978, p. 92.

good standing in the Church. What can be so dangerous about wealth? Furthermore, pleasures are good. God made them. Why all the blood and thunder about enjoying the benefits of one's hard work, benefits implanted in God's very handiwork? A book promoting poverty must be onesided.

These people, thinking of religion only in terms of benevolence and harmony, cannot bring themselves to reflect on the God of supreme holiness and justice. God is always the God of heaven, never of hell. They argue that

> we need not alarm ourselves,—that God is a merciful God,— that amendment is quite sufficient to atone for our offenses,— that though we have been irregular in our youth, yet that is a thing gone by,—that we forget it, and therefore God forgets it,—that the world is, on the whole, very well disposed towards religion,—that we should avoid enthusiasm,—that we should not be over serious,—that we should have large views on the subject of human nature,—and that we should love all men. This indeed is the creed of shallow men in *every* age.[3]

Practice Supposes Premises

Our purpose at the moment is to delve into premises. Political practices and religious teachings cannot be understood except in terms of their root presuppositions. The practical running of a state makes sense only in the light of the assumptions of the people. Revolutions happen not only because policies are unjust but also because radical philosophies differ. Policies flow out of premises. The same is true of religion. Buddhist theory is consistent with its agnostic position a propos of God. Protestantism must accept

---

[3] John Henry Newman, *Parochial and Plain Sermons*, I, sermon 24 (San Francisco: Ignatius Press, 1997), p. 204.

the fragmenting consequences of private judgment, and Catholic canon law reflects its acceptance of the divine origin of the hierarchical Church.

One badly misunderstands Gospel poverty if he views it as nothing more than a humanistic concern for the downtrodden or as a politico-sociological effort to redistribute the world's resources. The more a man studies evangelical poverty, the more he is struck by the elaborate yet consistent intertwining of doctrinal themes with actual practice.

Our immediate problem is not to show these intertwinings. That I shall do further on. Our real difficulty is the human propensity to judge by sympathies, not by evidence. I fear that some readers will admit the intertwinings during their encounter with these pages but then revert to merely human presuppositions as they continue on through the rest of the book in its practical applications to the various states in life. It is not easy for us to learn that God's thoughts are not our thoughts and his ways are not ours.

In lecture work I have found that I may explain at length and, I think, with clarity, radical revealed premises and then find that when we get to the nitty-gritty applications, some listeners have reverted to their own prosaic premises. Naturally enough, their conclusions are at variance with mine. What is still more disturbing is that many of these people seem unaware that they have either forgotten the revealed roots of the matter (though I had developed them twenty minutes earlier) or that their position is inconsistent with those roots. What concerns me is that this chapter may be forgotten as we work through the later ones.

Nonetheless, we hope for the best and present the New Testament premises undergirding its teaching on the use and misuse of material goods. Once these are granted, the rest of this volume makes perfect sense. Nothing else does.

Our first revealed presupposition: our destiny is literally out of this world. Eye has not seen, nor ear heard; indeed, it cannot even dawn on our unaided imagination the unspeakable delight God has prepared for those who love him (1 Cor 2:9). Before this destiny all worldly glitter is dull, all tinsel is cheap, all adventure is prosaic, all attraction is unsatisfying. I am well aware that this kind of language strikes some people as pious puff. Though one could prove that it is as solid as granite, I shall not do so. People who best know from experience, the saints, have said it far better than I ever could. The doubter should study before he rejects. If he studies and is of good will, he will not reject. Be that as it may, I merely assert the New Testament premise: nothing, absolutely nothing on the face of the earth compares with the advanced possession of God in deep prayer. We understand the Christic teaching on material goods only when we understand this.

Premise number two follows on the first: in this new era happiness is found not in eating and drinking this or that but in personal goodness and in the peace and joy given by the Holy Spirit (Rom 14:17). We are to rejoice in the Lord always, not simply occasionally (Phil 4:4). A consumerist society assumes quite the contrary. One needs only to read its advertising to be convinced of it—which is one reason it is easier for a camel to enter the eye of a needle than for a rich man to enter the kingdom of heaven (Mk 10:25). The New Testament assumes that happiness is found not in things but in persons and especially in the Divine Persons.

And this suggests our third presupposition: we are to be head over heels in love for God. We are to be so in love that we sing to him in our hearts always and everywhere (Eph 5:19-20). Every fiber of our being, heart, soul, and mind, is to become wholly love (Lk 10:27). People in love are not much concerned with things. They are person orientated, not thing centered. A consumerist is not in love.

Our fourth premise can be said in one word, asceticism. A genteel, soft, comfortable existence is foreign to the New Testament, because for wounded men and women it is foreign to being in love. Only those can love sincerely who are entirely purified by the word, detached from things less than God (1 Pet 1:22–23). Saint John of the Cross writes so much about detachment because he writes so much about supreme love. Saint Paul has the same message: only on condition that we crucify all self-indulgent desires can we belong to Christ Jesus (Gal 5:24). Hence it is no objection to revealed doctrine on factual poverty to say that it is difficult and requires sacrifice. Of course. They who want no part of asceticism want no part of love.

Our next premise follows hard on the last: no one can serve God and mammon (Lk 16:13). We must make a choice, and the choice cannot be fence straddling. The pharisees laughed at this (Lk 16:14), but they have never been noted for authenticity. The Gospel offers no comfort to those who wish to keep a foot in each of two worlds. Its teaching on the use of material things supposes that we are theists, that we have chosen God, that we are not compromisers.

And this implies a sixth presupposition: totality of pursuit. Nowhere in Scripture are we asked for much or most or quite a bit. Always it is everything. The God of revelation is never a God of fractions. It is not enough to love him with 95 percent of our heart, not enough to be detached from major obstacles, not enough to be merely cordial and helpful in community, not enough to be regular in prayer. No, we are to love with a whole heart, to be detached from all we possess, to enjoy a complete communal unity, to pray always (Mt 22:37; Lk 14:33; Jn 17:23; Lk 18:1). Merely human writers and speakers commonly dilute the totality of the divine message. Saints do not. The reader may note throughout this volume that what is said is what the saints literally and totally live. They embrace not only all these premises but the conclusions as well. This premise in particular, totality of pursuit, lies behind the radicality of New Testament teaching on poverty. Biblical men and women were by no means half-hearted or lukewarm.

Premise number seven: a consuming concern for the kingdom (Jn 4:34). Things are not the main business of life. They are means, only means. An artist eagerly absorbed in his work can skip a meal without noticing that he has not eaten. Geniuses often care little about their dress, perhaps at times too little, but their reason is magnanimous: they have something large on their minds, and they see clothing styles as of only marginal importance. Jesus and those who first wrote about him had the largest of minds. They were absorbed in the Father and his business. They were free of our pettiness, our concern with trivialities. They tried to raise our minds from the things of earth to those of heaven (Col 3:1-2).

This in turn suggests our next premise: we are all of us strangers on earth. We are nomads, pilgrims in search of our real fatherland in heaven (Heb 11:13-16). We entered the world with nothing, and we will leave it with nothing; we are therefore content with mere necessities (1 Tim 6:7-8). We do not think the things of earth important (Phil 3:19), but we await the resurrection in which we will see the real value of our bodies transfigured after the manner of the risen Jesus (Phil 3:20-21). In this light cosmetics and jewelry are seen to be poor substitutes for the real thing.

This pilgrim status implies still another presupposition: we are brothers and sisters to our fellow pilgrims, and we spontaneously, unquestioningly share good things with them.

Companions on earthly pilgrimage when they become more and more of one mind in their pursuit of the Holy One do not think twice about sharing their common resources. They gladly and readily make available their food and drink with others in the party. Saint James calls dead a faith that does not share its possessions (Jas 2:14–17).

Our final premise flows from all the others: understanding Gospel poverty perfectly requires a perfect conversion, a 180-degree switch from worldliness. One reason it is easier for a camel to enter the eye of a needle than it is for a rich man to attain heaven is that the latter is blinded by his clingings. He not only does not do what he ought to do with his wealth, he does not even see what he ought to do. To him it is obvious that his barns bursting with crops are to be used for his own pleasure: eat, drink, make merry, take things easy (Lk 12:16–21). It does not occur to him that this abundance should be shared with the downtrodden. Saint Paul tells the Romans (12:2) that the only way to know the perfect will of God is to undergo conversion from a worldly outlook. The sensual person cannot understand the things of the Spirit; it is nonsense to him (1 Cor 2:14). Unless one is attempting to lead a serious prayer life, he is not likely to be much affected by the message in these pages. There may be a momentary impact, but I would expect little by way of lasting results. I would suggest, therefore, that you, the reader, insert prayer into this reading. And more: if you are not now committed to a regular, serious prayer life, I would urge you to begin such today. Not next year, next month, not "when I feel better" or "when I will have more time and less work". Today.

A word of logic. If you accept the premises in this chapter, you will have no trouble with the remainder of this book. There is an inner consistency throughout the whole. If, on the other hand, you do not accept one or another premise, I would suggest that you stop now and get busy with prayer. These premises are not my private opinion. They are God's revealed word. And his word has the last word. If I accept his word, it heals and saves and enthralls me. If I reject it, it will condemn me. After you and I have faced him in serious prayer we are ready for the Gospel message about material goods.

PART II

VALUES: WHAT AND WHY?

5

What Gospel Poverty Is Not

Half the controversies in the world are verbal ones; and could they be brought to a plain issue, they would be brought to a prompt termination. Parties engaged in them would then perceive, either that in substance they agreed together, or that their difference was one of first principles. . . . When men understand each other's meaning, they see, for the most part, that controversy is either superfluous or hopeless.[1]

Such is the case with evangelical poverty. Supposing that the term *evangelical* means what it says, namely, Gospel, reasonably intelligent people can basically agree about its meaning by a careful study of the New Testament. Many of the dozens of questions, problems, disagreements I sketched in Chapter 2 are due chiefly to differing definitions of poverty. Clearing up concepts therefore is one-half of the battle.

The other half is the question of first principles. Even if you can through intellectually rooted evidence force a person to admit that your definition is the only founded one, it does not automatically follow that he will accept your message, buy your product. Especially is this true when the object of concern deals with one's style of life. People with fundamentally different principles interpret the same evidence in opposite senses. They may finally agree about

[1] John Henry Newman, *Oxford University Sermons*, sermon 10.

definitions, but most likely they will not agree about matters of validity and acceptability. I may cite one example. If one man holds that human prestige and bodily comfort are primary values in life, while another is convinced that humility and sacrifice are far more important, their views of frugality are going to be poles apart. Until there is basic conversion, further discussion is hopeless.

In this chapter we are concerned with concepts and definitions. Whether the reader and writer are sufficiently converted to accept the Gospel teaching that will follow is between each of us and God. I shall suppose that conversion without discussing it. Our first task then is to sketch clearly what the evangelical ideal is not. Establishing negatives differs from establishing positives. That Gospel poverty is not any of the following will be seen when, as we proceed through following chapters, we deal with what the positive evidences are. We now ask simply what Gospel poverty is not.

1 *Carelessness, disorder, laziness, or dirt.* Because the factually impoverished often lack incentive or education or proper home training, they sometimes live in unnecessary squalor. We may then easily assume that a lack of efficiency or tidiness is somehow bound up with the ideal of frugality. From seeing in the mass media so frequently the coexistence of filth and poverty, we easily infer an inner connection between them. There is no basis in the New Testament for this connection.

2 *Destitution.* By destitution we mean here the lack of the basic necessities for a decent human life. Rather than promote the idea of destitution, the Gospel requires that we share with the needy, that we rub it out wherever it exists. Hence, ordinarily we do not embrace destitution for ourselves. I say ordinarily because it could and does sometimes happen that a person is called by God to choose dire cir-

cumstances as a comforting identification with brothers and sisters who are forced so to live. Saint Benedict Joseph Labre was so called.

3 *Miserliness.* Avarice is a vice, not a virtue. Miserliness is actually opposed to evangelical frugality. The miser loves money so much that he is reluctant to part with it either for his own or others' benefits. The frugal person has no love for money. He sees it purely as the means it is, and he is happy to part with it, especially when he can benefit his neighbor.

4 *Economy.* Economy is a careful use of money and material goods, and as I take it here, it is a quality, not a defect. While it is often allied with a factually frugal style of living, economy is not identical with the Gospel ideal. One can be economical for a good reason (for example, to save money for other more important uses) or for a bad reason (for example, to deny to another what he needs). The latter is stinginess and of course not a virtue. One who is living the New Testament teaching will usually be economical in his use of creation, but it may possibly happen that what is more economical in a given case may be less in accord with Gospel poverty. An expensive, heavy car may last as long as two small ones, and thus be more "economical", but it does not follow that people with a vow of poverty ought to buy the former.

5 *Detachment (merely).* There is no doubt that detachment, inner freedom, unclutteredness are conditions for complete love of God and neighbor. Nor is there any doubt that the spirit of poverty is one of the results of factual poverty embraced in faith. Nor is it debatable that detachment brings about a sparing-sharing lifestyle. If it did not, it would be unreal, an illusion. Yet for all this, it remains true that the New Testament is not content with a spirit of poverty. This

detachment is indispensable, but more is needed before we
have satisfied the demands of the Lord Jesus.

6 *Availability of person, talent, time.* Apparently in an attempt
to meet the objection that few Christians of any vocation are
living a Gospel frugality on a voluntary basis, it has been sug-
gested that we change the definition to what we can more easily live, namely, an availability to others. In this concept a person
is poor when he gives to others his person, his talents, his time.
While this self-donation is no doubt praiseworthy, solving problems by changing definitions is hardly an honorable proce-
dure. If we are not living evangelical teaching, it is we who
should change, not the teaching. A mere reading of the New
Testament rapidly shows that when revelation speaks of poverty, it is speaking of material goods, not personal availability.
Our following chapters will make this abundantly clear.

7 *Insensitivity to beauty or health.* Scripture nowhere advises
us to be careless regarding health. True enough, there is no
support either for pampering one's body. We are to carry
our cross daily, but this does not imply that we abuse the
health God has given us. Even the Lord himself requires the
disciples to get rest when they need it after laborious work
(Mk 6:30–32). Likewise, we read nowhere in the sacred word
that we should pay no attention to the sublime beauties with
which the Creator has graced his universe. On the contrary,
we pray that our eyes be opened to the marvels of his hand
(Ps 119:18). It is he who gives light that we be enabled to
appreciate the splendors of his creation (Sir 17:7–8). The
patron of poverty, Saint Francis of Assisi, sang to the glories
of his "brothers and sisters" in subhuman creation. The person who looks upon and uses material things in accordance
with their genuine purpose grows in sensitivity to their real
value and beauty.

8 *Respectful use of creation.* Supposing that a Christian should be sensitive to created beauty, some conclude that the Gospel ideal of poverty is adequately met when we use God's gifts in a sober, respectful manner. No one questions that we should use the earth's resources soberly and respectfully, but this does not itself answer another question: Given the wholeness of our human situation, what is a respectful, sober use? Given the dire straits of the third and fourth worlds, given the fact of our native self-centeredness, and given our proclivity to cling to what we use and to use more than we need, what are sobriety and respect? The most selfish people can easily convince themselves that their use is "sober and respectful".

9 *Amorphous sentimentalism.* Wealthy societies do not lack people who can speak eloquently about the third and fourth worlds, who call emphatically for "consciousness raising" about the dire destitution among vast populations and yet who seem to see no incompatibility between their speech and their own way of life. They live comfortably, sometimes elegantly. They possess extensive wardrobes, enjoy costly vacations and recreations and dining and drinking and traveling. And yet they talk of the value of Gospel poverty. Their rhetoric of course impresses few listeners. One can only wonder if it is all to them a formless sentimentality. In any event the Gospel envisions hard facts, not empty rhetoric. Talking about the needy and yet not sharing with them betrays a dead faith (Jas 2:14–17) and an absence of love (1 Jn 3:17–18). Beatification and canonization processes make plain what the Church thinks of laymen and clerics and religious who live comfortable lives with scarcely a thought for the have-nots in our world. She makes it plain by her decisions as to who is finally canonized and who is not.

6

Emptiness and Radical Readiness

Sensible people do not choose emptiness for the sake of emptiness. Of itself negation has no value. It is literally nothing and is worth nothing. Reality is made to be and to be full. Silence has no value in itself, for it is a mere no talking.

The value of negative things derives, must derive, from something positive, something they make possible. Certain types of silence have great worth, because the omission of trivial talk may enable me to read a superb book or to converse with a gifted person or to get some needed rest or to commune with God. Factual poverty is a negation, a not having of certain material goods. Since it possesses no value in itself, its high commendation in the biblical revelation must derive from what it makes possible. The next four chapters develop the four main values of factual poverty.

First we must again note that the New Testament has some remarkably hard sayings about the incompatibility of riches and the kingdom. Humanly the two cannot be combined, since it is easier for a camel to pass through a needle's eye than for a rich man to enter God's kingdom (Mk 10:25 and parallels). Only God can work the transformation that will enable this wealthy person to give away what he does not need. The rich man who does not share with the beggar Lazarus at his gate ends up in hell, for he had his comfort in this life (Lk 16:19–31). No one can serve two masters; he must take his pick: God or money; he cannot have both (Mt 6:24). The word of God is smothered, choked, and does not reach maturity in people who succumb to cares, pleasures, and wealth (Lk 8:14 and parallels). We are to avoid avarice in all its forms, for there is no security in finite things even when we have an abundance of them (Lk 12:15). "Woe to the wealthy" is Jesus' proclamation to the rich, for they have their consolation now (Lk 6:24). We are not to lay up treasures on earth where moths and rust corrode and thieves steal. Our treasure is to be in heaven, in God, our new center of gravity (Mt 6:19–21).

Why so dim a view of wealth? Why so value a not having, a mere negative? The Gospel's first answer: poverty bestows not simply an abstract ideal but a concrete experience. It gives the poor man the experience of a radical readiness for the kingdom. What does this really mean?

First the concept of readiness. Readiness is a nothing-something. We may suppose two five-year-old youngsters, one of whom is said to be ready for reading, the other not. Presumably neither can actually read. The first one's readiness to learn reading is a "nothing" in the sense that there is right now no reading skill. Yet it is also a something in that he has a degree of maturity sufficient to enable him to absorb instruction when it is given to him. The other youngster labors under a nothing-nothing. Not only does he lack reading skills; he also lacks the maturity needed to absorb instruction and to profit from it.

One is ready for the kingdom when he is so intellectually and morally developed by a love for truth and goodness that when he hears the revealed word he can react positively to it. He is sensitive to its beauty, attractiveness, authenticity. There are, of course, degrees of readiness and unreadiness for the kingdom. As Jesus puts it in his parable of the sower, there are those who yield nothing and others who yield thirty-fold or sixtyfold or a hundredfold. Sensitivity to truth and goodness is a major reason why in a parish church on a Sunday morning there are so many widely diverse reactions even to a good homily. The saint may fall into ecstacy upon hearing the simple mention of God's goodness, while the sinner may remain as cold as a stone before the eloquence of a Lacordaire.

The sensitivity or readiness we are talking about is radical. Factual poverty embraced in faith does something to a person in the deep resources of his being. It matures him, develops him, makes him receptive to what the Lord Jesus is about. It is not merely a superficial ability to parrot words about the dire straits of the third and fourth worlds, to proclaim with an abundance of rhetoric but with no follow through in life.

Further, this readiness is an experience, not merely an abstract ideal. One who is poor in and for the Lord is concretely affected by the Gospel. Yes, he may well know an abstract ideal, but he also resonates with it in daily life. He is on God's wavelength.

What do we mean by kingdom in this context? We mean the new era revealed in the risen Christ. We mean the new creation proclaimed by Saint Paul. We mean the transference of our center of gravity from the finitude of this world to the infinitude of the bosom of the Trinity. We mean what Jesus stands for, what he proclaims of his Father, of himself, and of their common Spirit. We mean what eye has not seen nor ear heard, what cannot be imagined by our prosaic minds.

Such is the meaning of the expression, experience of a radical readiness for the kingdom. Factual frugality embraced willingly in faith bestows on one not a mere abstract, pale awareness. It brings about a felt sensitivity to what the

Lord Jesus is all about. It helps dissolve opaqueness, dullness, resistance to the word of God.

It must be noticed that the values of the kingdom are just about 180 degrees removed from the values of the world. "My thoughts are not your thoughts, and my ways are not your ways." Indeed they are not. To get the feel for this all one needs to do is to read the morning paper next to the Gospel. What are the world's basic values? Advertising makes them clear, especially when we notice the unexpressed, fundamental premises that underlie 98 percent of the messages. These premises are so taken for granted that no one feels any need to explain or promote them. It is assumed that everyone knows them and that most people live by them. What are these premises: prestige is a primary value . . . bodily comfort and pleasure are indispensable . . . this life is all we have, so let's enjoy it to the full . . . impressing people with one's possessions and accomplishments and attractiveness is important . . . sexual excitement and satisfaction are crucial . . . success is "coming out on top" in relation to others . . . money is a must, for without it one can have very little of anything else worth having in life.

If we turn to the pages of the New Testament we find a picture as opposite as it could be: humility, being last, unknown, hidden in Christ, is a condition for getting into the kingdom . . . prestige is worthless and even an obstacle to greatness . . . the hard road and the narrow gate, carrying the cross every day is immensely important . . . dying to our selfishness and crucifying our illusory desires are indispensable . . . impressing people is of no importance at all, whereas being pleasing to the divine eyes is everything . . . virginity is a favored and privileged state, and chaste fidelity in marriage mirrors the very union of Christ and his Church . . . one may not try to best others; rather he is to serve them as though he were a slave . . . it is most difficult, indeed it is humanly impossible, for the wealthy to enter the kingdom of heaven.

It takes little imagination to see that one who freely chooses to be poor is far more prepared to understand the previous paragraph than one who is surrounded with luxury, comfort, pleasures of sense, who basks in prestige and position, who lives only for the good opinion of other human beings. The difference is like that of a paper towel and wax paper in their receptivity and resistance to water. Just as there are hundreds of differing degrees of reaction to water among types and qualities of paper, so it is with human beings and the divine word.

I should now like to say this in biblical terms. Detachment is one-half of this readiness; humility is the other. Poverty is related to both.

They are in a blessed, happy condition who are poor in spirit, for they have the kingdom of heaven (Mt 5:3). The detached *anawim*, the little ones, are so ready for the kingdom that they already somehow possess it. All of us are to be so uncluttered that we resemble the lilies of the field and the birds of the air. Unlike pagans, who know not where they are going and thus are concerned about food and drink and clothing, the disciples are to be free of these worries and set their hearts on the kingdom before all else (Mt 6:25–34). One must renounce all that he possesses as a condition for belonging to Jesus (Lk 14:33). He must mind not the things on earth but those of heaven (Col 3:1–2). The early faithful not only were resigned to being stripped of their possessions; they rejoiced at their lot, for they knew that they had something better and lasting. They had the fatherland with the risen Lord as their destiny (Heb 10:34).

That there is a connection between factual frugality and detachment is clear. We ask next: Why is it so? The answer

is that for us wounded human beings, possessing impercep-
tibly slips into being possessed. No sooner do I have a watch
of some quality than I begin to be reluctant to part with it
even if someone needs it more than I do. This means that it,
a mere thing, has taken a hold on my heart. It is not only the
miser who is possessed by his money. He is merely a strong
case of all of us who are less than saints. One of the most
rapid ways to upset a man is to suggest that he ought to part
with the superfluous material things he enjoys. Rare, too, is
the woman who takes readily to the idea that her jewelry or
extensive wardrobe should be disposed of for the benefit of
the poor. Having wealth is damaging to the pursuit of the
kingdom because the very having does something to one's
inner life, one's very ability to love God for his own goodness and others in and for him. This must be at the core of
why Jesus proclaimed that it is easier for a camel to pass
through the eye of a needle than for a rich man to enter
heaven.

If detachment is one-half of what readiness for the kingdom means, humility is the other. Unless we are converted
and become as little as a child, there is no possibility of getting to God (Mt 18:1–4). If I am filled with myself, married
to my own ideas and ways of doing things, convinced that
somehow I am the hub of the universe, there is of course no
room in me for being filled with God, for accepting or even
desiring his wisdom, for making him my center of gravity.
Indeed, sensitivity to the divine is dependent on humility.

And poverty has a great deal to do with humility. We human beings tend to equate our level of to be with our level
of to have. The more we possess, the more we are—in our
own minds. The man with a large estate, several cars, a sizable portfolio just assumes that he is superior to the slum-
dweller. The woman who is seldom seen in the same dress is

sure that she ranks higher in human society than the dowdy wife whose family is on welfare. Perhaps the chief reason prestige is so immensely important to many people is that the impression they make on others dictates their own value. And an abundance of material things, in their opinion, enhances their prestige. They are living as slaves in the minds of others. Being subject to human evaluations, they are little inclined to the divine.

People who by choice embrace a frugal lifestyle assess themselves far more realistically than those who do not. They are free from a subjection to the minds of others. They know of their intrinsic worth before God and do not feel a need for the shoddy props afforded by mere things. Being innerly uncluttered, they are ready for the divine invasion. It easily happens.

A few real-life illustrations may help. Saint John Chrysostom calmly endured exile as recompense for his fidelity to the Gospel and the Church. Said he,

> What are we to fear? Death? "Life to me means Christ, and death is gain." Exile? "The earth and its fullness belong to the Lord." The confiscation of our goods? "We brought nothing into this world, and we shall surely take nothing from it." I have only contempt for the world's threats, I find its blessings laughable. I have no fear of poverty, no desire for wealth.[1]

To Gabriele of Volterra, a Franciscan who lived in an elegant manner even though he was considered the greatest scholar and preacher in the order of his time, Saint Catherine of Siena was not hesitant to declare, "How is it possible for you to understand anything of that which pertains to the

---

[1] *Ante exsilium*, in *The Liturgy of the Hours*, Sept. 13.

kingdom of God, you who live only for the world?" So force-
ful was she with him that he arranged on the spot to give his
accumulations to the poor.[2] Saint Thomas More, recounted
his friend Erasmus, throughout his life drank nothing but
cold water. With a typical touch of humor Thomas berated
people who cared much about the elegance of their clothes:
"How many a man is proud of the woolen cloak on his back,
not remembering that it was on a sheep's back before it was
on his."[3] This love for elegance and for money has a pecu-
liar deadening effect in the spiritual life. Saint Philip Neri
used to remark that it is far easier to convert a lustful person
to God than a covetous one.[4]

This radical readiness for the kingdom is, then, the first
reason Jesus declared that the poor in fact are in so blessed a
condition. No matter whether they are married or virgin, if
so blessed, they enjoy an inbuilt sensitivity and receptivity to
the mind and heart of God.

[2] Johannes Jorgensen, *Saint Catherine of Siena*, trans. Ingebord Lund (Lon-
don: Longmans Green, 1938), p. 146.

[3] Daniel D. Donovan, *Homiletic and Pastoral Review*, Nov., 1979, p. 49.

[4] Theodore Maynard, *Mystic in Motley: The Life of St. Philip Neri* (Milwaukee: Bruce Publishing, 1946), p. 158.

7

A Sparing-Sharing Lifestyle

Words are cheap, actions costly. The world is full of people who talk about "community". Dressed in the latest styles, men and women, religious as well as lay, are eloquent in their grand statements and convention resolutions about securing justice in the world. We see on television screens and in news magazines pictures of babies who are not much more than skin-covered skeletons, and we solemnly pronounce how wretched and tragic it all is. Yet we continue with our energy-consuming cars, our extravagant amusements, expensive vacations, unneeded traveling, lavish wardrobes, elegant drinking and dining.

Yes, words are cheap, and many of us abound in them. Saints are quite the opposite: they say little, do much. They are aware of the New Testament's demand that if we see even one brother in need but close our heart to him, we cannot be loving God, that we are to love not simply in word but also in action (1 Jn 3:17–18). Toward the end of this chapter we shall see this doctrine in action, but for now we must first lay some foundations in the contemporary world and then in the word of God.

Signs of the Times

The literature of our day is replete with statistics that declare the gross inequities among nations of the world in the use of our planet's resources. Since these facts and figures vary somewhat from one decade to another, we may be content to report approximate proportions. In recent times the first world has had a gross national product per capita of about three times that of the second world, about five or six times that of third world countries, and well over 20 times that of fourth world countries. Referring to the financial condition of citizens in developing countries, Robert McNamara has rightly observed that mere numbers can by no means give us an adequate appreciation of their wretched circumstances. "But what is beyond the power of any set of statistics to illustrate is the inhuman degradation the vast majority of these individuals are condemned to . . . Malnutrition saps their energy, stunts their bodies and shortens their lives." He goes on to observe that the poverty could be alleviated no little bit by "a comparatively small contribution in money and skills from the developed world".[1]

The problem is not merely global. Gross inequities are found in one and the same nation, even in prosperous nations. Nor is the problem merely secular and civil. Religious spokesmen who speak but do not live compassion are considered by the world's deprived ones to be sounding brass and tinkling cymbals. Some years ago in Bogota, during the second Inter-American Conference of Religious Superiors, the South American delegation bluntly told the North American representatives that "your lifestyle belies your rhetoric". It is still true.

New Testament Premises

The clash between gospel teaching on the use of God's creation and the factual situation in our twenty-first century is

[1] *Time*, June 4, 1979, p. 24.

stark. The clash is stark because the two sets of premises could hardly be more different. The world's principles are either explicitly or implicitly I-centered; The Gospel's principles are we-in-God centered. The difference in consequences is vast. The New Testament supposes, for example, that all men and women are my brothers and sisters. (I have counted at least 209 uses of the words *brother* and *sister* in the New Testament.) Jesus and Paul and the others all suppose that our graced brotherly-sisterly relationship in him is far more important than blood relationships. We are expected to act toward all our new associates as we ideally would act toward our immediate blood-related family members (1 Pet 1:22–23).

Of course, this sounds pious enough, and what Christian will deny it? The trouble is that few who admit it in theory are at all prepared to live it in fact. One need only to consider how differently we react when we hear that our blood sister or brother needs a meal and when we hear that someone in Afghanistan is dying of starvation. We react immediately in the first case, probably not at all in the second. But in any event the New Testament assumes that we are indeed one family by grace blood, and it draws the logical consequences, consequences so radical that almost no one lives them fully.

To appreciate the second revealed premise I must get a bit philosophical for a moment. Material goods (knives, books, computers, libraries, chapels, clothing) are extensions of our persons. A knife extends our persons as beings who shape and cut material things for our own needs. Books reflect the fact that we are intellectual beings with ideas to share with one another. A chapel declares that we are worshipping beings who wish to engage in adoration and prayer together and in a sacred place. Clothing not only warms our bodies but also declares to others who we are and what we think of ourselves.

Biblical writers were not philosophers, but they knew well enough that material sharing is a consequence of any sincere love. If the goods of earth are extensions of my person and if I love my neighbor as myself, I naturally share my good things. It is idle for me to proclaim concern for the poor, the homeless, for example, and at the same time indulge in elegant dining and drinking, pleasure traveling, and an extensive wardrobe. My life belies my rhetoric.

The third New Testament premise is a corollary of the second. We share with the needy to the point of a rough equality. If I am to love my fellowman as myself, it must follow that I desire that his needs be cared for at least as well as I care for mine. To desire otherwise is not to love him as I love myself.

Our final premise: poverty of spirit is not enough. Availability to others is not enough. A respectful use of creation is not enough. All these are good, of course. They are also convenient and easy prey to rationalization. People who pamper themselves with luxuries can readily convince themselves that they are detached from all they so abundantly use, that they are indeed available to others, that they are dealing with creation respectfully. Not many believe them, but they do believe themselves. In any event, the Gospel demands factual sharing and not mere words.

Four New Testament Traditions

The first-century followers of Jesus were unanimous in their deeply rooted conviction that a genuine disciple absolutely must share his material possessions with the needy. One clear, properly exegeted text would be enough to establish the obligation, but we have no less than four traditions that completely coincide. The first is from Luke. When John the Baptist in no uncertain terms demands from the crowd conversion as a preparation for the coming Messiah, the listeners ask what they must do. From the hundreds of precepts in the Old Testament that John could have cited as proof of conversion, he picks the sharing precept: if a person has two tunics and his brother none, he must give one away—and the same with food (Lk 3:10–11). One of the key traits of the ideal Church is that the disciples share all things in common: they sold their property and cared for everyone's needs from their pooled resources (Acts 2:44–46). In one and the same breath Luke describes how these early Christians were of one heart and mind and held everything in common (Acts 4:32–35). He seems to be saying in concrete terms that material sharing is an extension of inner love, inner oneness of heart.

Paul proclaims the same message. The Apostle speaks in glowing terms of the Macedonians, who despite their stark poverty begged him insistently for the favor of sharing with fellow Christians not only from superfluity but even from their need (2 Cor 8:1–5). Paul does not expect that the Corinthians go quite that far, but he does expect them to share to the extent that they and the needy community may enjoy an equality in their use of material goods (2 Cor 8:13–15). Even though this is surely the most radical social doctrine on the face of planet Earth (communism is by no means this radical), it is a logical conclusion from the premise that as members of one and the same family we love one another as ourselves. To say that I love another and then refuse to share (to the extent of this rough equality) is mere rhetoric. I have the words of love but not the deeds. This obligation of openhandedness with the needy is mentioned also in Romans 12:13 and Hebrews 13:16.

James uses vigorous language and a concrete illustration to make the same point. If some brother or sister in the community suffers an insufficiency of food and clothing and another extends to that person a cheery good wish unaccompanied with a gift of these bare necessities, the well wisher's faith is dead (Jas 2:14–17). Strong words. But true.

The joannine tradition bears the same blunt message: if a person of means sees a needy disciple but closes his heart to him, that person cannot be loving God. Apparently we have here a serious sin that destroys the life of grace. John does not say simply that this tight-fisted individual is not loving God; he cannot be loving God, for love is not mere talk—it is living and active (1 Jn 3:17–18).

At this point in our discussion I could understand that the careful reader may be disturbed, deeply disturbed. How many, he may ask himself, do what these four New Testament traditions require? This question seems to imply another: How many who realize this obligation are in the state of love and grace?

No doubt this is serious. Yet more must be said. The contemporary teaching Church has made the point more than once that it is not enough to give of our superfluities to the needy of our world. We are to give even from our need. This is still more rare. Pope John Paul II during his visit to the United States in 1979 laid it down that we are not merely to share with the world's indigent from what we have left over, from the crumbs that fall from our tables, but from what we need; Vatican Council II offered the same teaching twice in *Gaudium et spes*, nos. 69 and 88. Before one dismisses all this as an extreme exaggeration, he would do well to reflect first. If we love our brother as ourselves, and if he suffers a more radical need than we, surely we will relieve his dire necessity from our lesser one. The real problem is not in the logic of the matter; it is whether we actually love our neighbor as ourselves.

A sharing manner of life is not optional. Creation belongs to all members of the human race, not mainly to the clever, intelligent, resourceful, well born. Sheer justice demands equitable participation. Pope Paul VI cited Saint Ambrose when he said,

> You are not making a gift of your possessions to the poor person. You are handing over to him what is his. For what has been given in common for the use of all you have arrogated to yourself. The world is given to all and not only to the rich.[2]

A word of caution. In all our enthusiasm for the alleviation of the plight of the poor we are well advised to avoid the basically atheistic thesis that material destitution is the greatest of all evils. Our enthusiasm for economic equity and a just distribution of the world's resources can only too easily lead us to assume that the greatest poverty is material rather than spiritual. Man's greatest need is love, love for God and for brother and sister. We do not have here a lasting city. We are pilgrims plodding along to the fatherland, wayfarers on the way to home.

Social injustice is evil, no doubt. But there is far greater evil, namely, that of not seeking God. Liberation theology so focused on remedying this world's oppressions that it neglected the immeasurably greater oppression of failing to pursue our destiny of beatific vision in risen body. They who try to solve only the problem of material destitution offer the poor thin gruel. What does it profit a man, rich or poor, to gain the whole world if he suffers the loss of his soul?

No one, I trust, will understand our word of caution as negating what the rest of this volume contains. Small minds

---

[2] *Populorum progressio*, no. 23.

pit truth against truth; large minds do not. They of the largest minds, the saints, have lived heroically the sparing-sharing life of the Gospels, while at the same time they first of all sought eternal life both for themselves and for others.

Some, like Saint John the Baptist de la Salle, lived the message of this volume in a simple direct manner: they literally sold all they owned and gave the proceeds to the poor.[3] Others responded to the Gospel after the manner of Blessed Louisa Albertoni, who, after her husband died, lived in deepest personal poverty and prayer. This woman expended her entire fortune in behalf of the needy to the point that she had nothing left, and she herself lived on alms. Louisa had a unique way of getting rid of her wealth. She would bake huge batches of bread, put gold and silver coins in the loaves, and then distribute them to the poor.[4]

Other saints retained some of their property but used it extensively after the fashion demanded by Jesus himself: when we give a party, we should invite, not the well to do, not relatives and friends, but rather the downtrodden, the stranger, the destitute (Lk 14:12–14). Most people do quite the opposite of the Gospel injunction. But not the saints. While he was still a layman Saint Peter Damian not only gave directly to the needy but also often invited them to his own table and served them with his own hands.[5] Saint Paulinus of Nola and his wife used their wealth for sundry religious and philanthropic enterprises, but they also supported a large number of poor debtors, itinerants, and other needy people. Many of these they lodged in the lower section of their own house.[6]

[3] Butler, *Lives of the Saints*, 2:316.
[4] Ibid., 1:447.
[5] Ibid., 1:399–401.
[6] Ibid., 2:616.

Thomas Stapleton tells how Saint Thomas More, besides giving monetary gifts,

> very often invited his poorer neighbours to his table, receiving them graciously and familiarly. The rich were rarely invited, the nobility hardly ever. Moreover in his parish, Chelsea, he hired a house in which he placed many who were infirm, poor, or old, providing for them at his own expense.

Stapleton adds that as a lawyer Thomas gave his legal services free of charge to widows and orphans.[7] Saint Louis, King of France, daily had a large number of indigents for meals near the palace, and these he often served himself.[8]

Some of the saints went further still. During a desperate famine Saint Louis de Montfort repeatedly went out to beg food for the hordes of beggars who came to him.[9] While still a young man Saint Dominic sold his library to help the poor at Palencia.[10] Saint Vincent de Paul's public were society's rejects: beggars, galley slaves, prostitutes. He too begged food for them.[11]

Saint Robert Bellarmine gave a novel twist to all this. Not only did he share liberally with the poor, but when as a cardinal he had no more money to give, he would have his own belongings pawned in order to secure an alms. Among items pawned for the needy were his cardinal's ring and the mattress from his own bed. The cardinal even directed that the red serge hangings be taken down and given for clothing to

---

[7] E. E. Reynolds, *St. Thomas More* (New York: Doubleday Image edition), p. 151.

[8] Butler, 3:395, 397.

[9] Eddie Doherty, *Wisdom's Fool*, p. 162.

[10] Sheila Kaye-Smith, "St. Dominic", in *Saints and Ourselves*, ed. P. Caraman (New York: Doubleday Image edition), pp. 82–83.

[11] Igino Giordani, *St. Vincent de Paul*, pp. 128, 130.

some ragged urchins in the street. Robert's explanation: "The walls won't catch cold." [12]

The destitute, of course, need our love and caring more than they need our money. This too the saints did not overlook. Saint Vincent de Paul stood in reverence before the poor and looked on them as his masters. [13] Shabby beggars who came to Saint Robert Bellarmine were seated in the same chair used by visiting cardinals. James Brodrick, S.J., tells us that

> it was not merely what he gave, however, but his manner of giving that made St. Robert the idol of the unfortunate. He treated them as gentlemen, always standing and removing his cap when they came in. No matter how late might be the hour or how weary and worn he might be, there was a welcoming smile for them, and a patient ear for the longest of stories. He had no use for the platitudes of officialdom. It was enough for him that a fellow creature was cold or hungry or houseless. It was not his business to judge whether they were deserving, and his charity was of the authentic kind that thinks no evil, believes all things, hopes all things, endures all things. He had quite a good deal to endure for, of course, he was imposed upon and cheated again and again. . . . He had a fixed principle that it was better to be deceived a hundred times than miss one genuine case. [14]

Austere and hard on themselves, the saints are customarily indulgent and even tender with the ill and unfortunate. Saint Paschal Baylon, who as a layman went barefooted, ate meagerly and fasted often, yet went to the trouble of obtaining

---

[12] James Brodrick, *Robert Bellarmine*, pp. 164–65.
[13] Giordani, *St. Vincent de Paul*, p. 131.
[14] Brodrick, *Robert Bellarmine*, p. 166.

delicacies for the sick and needy.[15] Saint Teresa of Avila mentioned in one of her letters that she commonly gave away to others the candies and other niceties she received. Saint Catherine Labouré amazed her religious companions after her death when they found out the rigor of her personal poverty. Yet during the saint's beatification process one of the nuns recalled how sixty years earlier Catherine one day had obtained some warm flannel to keep the nun from catching cold after she had emerged from laundry work dampened by her duties.[16] Saint Philip Neri, ascetic that he was and with his burning love for God, ended his long oratory sermons with a program of classical music aimed at providing recreation and uplifting the participants.[17]

Yes, words are cheap, and many of us abound in them. Actions are costly, and the saints abound in them. Without action our faith is dead.

[15] Butler, 2:335.
[16] Joseph Dirvin, *St. Catherine Laboure*, p. 145.
[17] Theodore Maynard, *Mystic in Motley*, p. 130.

8

Apostolic Credibility

To be credible in our modern age a person must visibly demonstrate personal integrity in the small details of everyday life. Eminent politicians are not assumed to be authentic simply because they can give a rousingly good speech. One may be able to fool some of the people some of the time, but I doubt that mere words have ever moved the masses for long. In this day of the mass media, our daily deluge of words has further cheapened the value of mere talk.

If we wonder why, despite the millions of us who follow Christ, the world has not long ago been converted, we need not look far for one solution. We are not perceived as men on fire. We look too much like everyone else. We appear to be compromisers, people who say that they believe in everlasting life but actually live as though this life is the only one we have. A small band of men with deep convictions, burning convictions, went out into the first century and converted the then-known world. By the fourth century that world had been largely transformed.

One may object to this analysis by noting that not everyone accepted Jesus himself and that, therefore, there is something else operative besides example. True, no doubt. We are still infected with original sin, and there are people in any century so wounded and so self-centered that they will not accept the most persuasive proclamation even when it is delivered by a saint.

Yet our earlier observation remains true: men and women of goodwill are powerfully moved to God when they see before their eyes sheer Gospel goodness. I recall seeing on television, some years ago, a woman on a New York street on the verge of tears of joy as she expressed to the reporter how marvelous it was "to be so close to so holy a man". She had referred to Pope John Paul II, who had just passed by in a motorcade. Each of us has experienced, perhaps more times than once, the mighty impact heroic holiness makes when we see it unfold before our very eyes. It may be the quiet acceptance of an insult, the turning of the cheek. It may be the radiance of a simple person in deep prayer. It may be the extraordinary humility of a famous scholar. It may be the freely chosen poverty of one who comes from a wealthy family.

The main point in this chapter is not simply that example moves others to imitate what they have seen. At this moment our chief concern is credibility. Apostles are salesmen. They are selling something, and to sell one must persuade. To persuade, one must be believable.

This is where factual poverty comes in. Few things in human life demonstrate as rapidly as one's way of life what he is and what he really stands for. Talk is cheap; lived example is not. We tend to take seriously people who obviously are not promoting for their own benefit whatever it is they are promoting. In our modern newspapers, magazines, and electronic media, we are deluged with hundreds of advertisements every day and with thousands of words (the majority of our population has the television set on from four to six hours per day), and consequently a few more words in a class presentation or a homily are not going to sway many people unless they hear those words in the context of a life selflessly given to God and his people. As someone well put it, there is more influence with less affluence.

It comes as no surprise, therefore, that the Gospel had radical things to say about proclamation and the poverty of the proclaimer. Jesus instructs his representatives that on their missionary journey they are to take nothing but a staff—no bread, no haversack, no coins, no spare tunic (Mk 6:8–9; Mt 10:9–10; Lk 9:3; 10:4). This is the ideal, an ideal to be pursued when such is possible, when one can more or less count on the hospitality of those to whom one is ministering, an ideal concretized in some of the saints. Saint Francis Borgia, in his preaching travels, took the Gospel literally in that he carried no money with him, but only a little bag to hold the alms he would receive for his sustenance. He had of course no private carriage. He walked. In the course of these journeys it was Francis' rule to stay at night near a church, even if that meant sleeping under the stars or in a filthy inn. We are hardly surprised that this man in his vast popularity was mobbed by crowds and, like Saints Philip Neri and Francis Xavier (likewise astonishingly successful apostles), would fall into prolonged ecstacy during his celebration of Mass.[1]

Yet when the disciples go forth into a hostile world, the Lord does permit them to take along a purse, a haversack, and even a sword (Lk 22:35–36). This last text supposes that

the happy times of Jesus' ministry are over, when the apostolate was easy, when one needed nothing and lacked nothing. What would one have done with a purse or a traveling bag for provisions? But now, at the hour of Jesus' Passion, a new period begins. Now one cannot do without a purse or

[1] Margaret Yeo, *The Greatest of the Borgias*, pp. 166, 199, 210.

traveling bag, simply relying on people's hospitality. From now on, they can count not on hospitality but on hostility. The disciples, when attacked, would have to defend themselves; this is what the image of the sword suggests, which certainly has a symbolic value here.[2]

It is interesting how the Church, especially through the understanding of her saints, has well interpreted these texts, neither derogating from an austere poverty nor succumbing to a legalistic literalism.

Timothy, an apostolic man, is to rid himself of superfluities. Since he came into the world with nothing and will leave it with nothing, he is to be content with his food and clothing (1 Tim 6:7–8). After the example of Jesus himself (Lk 4:18), the Lord's messengers are to favor the poor in their labors (Gal 2:9–10; Jas 2:1–5). They give without charge (Mt 10:8), though, of course, they are to be cared for, since the laborer is worthy of his hire. They desire to have for themselves as little as possible (Acts 3:5–6; 2 Cor 6:4, 10), and they are as a matter of fact poor (Lk 9:2–3). They are willing to suffer deprivations (2 Cor 11:27; Phil 4:11–13), and they are glad to suffer redemptively (Col 1:24). It is not surprising that they transformed a terribly worldly world.

Not only are words without actions unimpressive to men of our day, but the very person who utters the words can incite disgust in perceptive listeners, who see a wide disparity between his life and speech. From England I once read the opinion that

> many a priest who now glibly preaches a "christian marxism" would have to forego the brandy and cigars he now enjoys at the rich man's table in between militant sermons in

---

[2] Jacques Dupont, in *Gospel Poverty*, trans. M. Guinan, pp. 45–46.

church and elsewhere. . . . If this sounds gratuitously unkind, it is because one is a little tired of such priests who, cosy in countries where civil wars are unlikely, preach revolution in the student milieu. Many of them would run a mile if they actually heard the whine of a bullet or had to salvage a child whose jaw had been blown off (which is the sort of thing that revolution means).[3]

We can make our point in still another way. The typical saint is vastly successful in sparking whole throngs to give up either mediocrity or dire sinfulness. One could not meet Saint Philip Neri without being struck with the unearthly charm of the man. He heard confessions for hours on end day and night, and he led large groups of men to give up the world to follow him as he became the apostle of Rome. I do not maintain that Philip's success in the apostolate was due solely to his poverty, for he was an immensely attractive person from the mere human point of view. But nonetheless his austerity was proof positive that his jokes—for which he was and is famous—were nothing trivial or superficial. After his own youthful "conversion", the saint's single daily meal consisted of bread, water, and a few vegetables. Before he went out to work for two years, he gave up whole days and nights to prayer. As a priest perhaps his chief problem was falling into ecstasy, so vehement was his love for God. The celebration of Mass would take him two hours. Sometimes before Mass, to quiet the vehemence of his love, he would read a page or two from a book of jokes he kept for that purpose.

The Curé of Ars, a simple parish priest in the midst of a previously negligent flock, drew thousands of people to his confessional. He did not, of course, advertise. His personal

[3] Hugh Kay, *The Way*, supplement no. 9, Spring, 1970, p. 72.

prayer-poverty impact was spread by word of mouth. His whole way of life itself shouted authenticity. Before the pilgrimages began as an institution, Saint John Vianney possessed only one well-patched cassock. Due to later pressures from others, he agreed to have two cassocks and no more. Gifts of a new one were always refused, and he preferred to wear the poorer of the two. If an extra new one was put into his room without his knowledge, he gave it away. For his dining utensils he was content with a bowl and a spoon, and his rectory was in a dilapidated condition. In order to give to the poor, he sold all personal property, including furniture and linen. In his later years "he was paying the rent for at least thirty families".[4]

Saint Vincent de Paul considered money a burden to apostolic men and women. To a priest he remarked that "we are not virtuous enough to carry the burden of plenty and of apostolic virtue, and I am afraid that we never shall be, and that the first will ruin the second". The saint asked the priests of the mission, "When every comfort is ours, are we real missionaries?" Because we "live by the sweat of the poor, we should work assiduously to be deserving of our upkeep".[5] Though Vincent was not called to the more extraordinary practices of poverty, he did live and proclaim the simple, austere frugality of honest labor, a frugality that underlined his sincerity and that of his priests and sisters.

Saint Francis Xavier was a living exemplar of the relationship between factual poverty and apostolic credibility. No surprise is it that the number of his conversions is legendary. This marvel of effectiveness and patron of missionaries lived as the people he served. He slept on the ground in a hut, and

[4] Francis Trochu, *The Cure d'Ars*, pp. 460, 462.
[5] Jacques Delarue, *The Holiness of Vincent de Paul*, pp. 99, 96–97.

he dined on rice and water.[6] His usual fare was "rice in one dreary form or another supplemented in good times with fish. ... He never seemed to care or even to know what he ate, or how little of it." He would sometimes go two days with almost no food. And this is the same man who would habitually spend most of the night in prayer, at most allowing himself on occasion two or three hours of sleep. One can get the feel for the otherworldly impression Xavier and his companions gave in Sakai, Japan, upon their arrival: "Barefooted ... swollen and torn feet ... intolerable cold ... poorly clad strangers ... such nondescripts as they ... cassocked scarecrows ... hungry and half frozen."[7]

Saint Dominic, who did heroic work in reclaiming heretics to the faith, advised a bishop who went about his apostolic visitation accompanied by a retinue of soldiers and servants: "The enemies of the faith cannot be overcome like that. Arm yourself with prayer, rather than a sword; wear humility rather than fine clothes."[8] Saint Bernard was of similar mind when it came to what kind of life an acclesiastic ought to have. Said he, "Though it be reasonable that one who serves the altar should live by the altar, yet it must not be to promote either his luxury or his pride. Whatever goes beyond bare nourishment and simple plain clothing is sacrilege and theft."[9] The saints do not mince words, nor do they take flight in ambiguous jargon.

Saint Charles Borromeo stands out in history as the model bishop in bringing about in real life the reform legislated by

---

[6] Butler, *Lives of the Saints*, 4:476.
[7] James Brodrick, *Saint Francis Xavier* (New York: Double Image edition), pp. 92, 254–55.
[8] Butler, 3:260.
[9] Ibid., 3:362.

the Council of Trent. Perhaps the main reason he was so successful in reforming the clergy was that he first reformed himself. Though he was a cardinal, he lived as a poor man in his private life. He once remarked that while he had to wear a cardinal's robes during the day, he would wear his single old tattered cassock in off hours at night. He chose to have no other either in winter or in summer.[10]

One who has read extensively in the lives of the saints knows well that these few examples are not unusual. They are routine instances of the constant picture: the saints make astonishing impressions on those with whom they come into contact. Whether they were naturally eloquent or not, the impact was there, and it was unmistakable. They were prodigiously effective in touching minds and hearts. Now this apostolic authenticity, this basic credibility is not only an externally observable phenomenon. It has internal roots. A man concerned with things is not concerned with the supernatural realm. As the Master himself put it, we cannot serve both God and mammon. It is one or the other, not both. We must make a choice. People, even worldly people, can easily pick up whether we are living for this world or the next. If our actions contradict our words, it is the former they believe.

The person who like Saint Augustine is panting after his Maker cannot long keep his light hidden even if he tries. If silent love is burning within, there will appear a disinterest in material things without. People will know that this man is interested in people, not in himself. They see the authenticity with their own eyes.

Men on fire are sparks in the stubble.

[10] Ibid., 4:257.

9

Pilgrim Witness

There is much in Scripture to which a theist has little difficulty in giving a theoretical assent but to which in concrete daily life he grants almost no assent at all. No convinced theist has any problem in admitting that idle talk is reprehensible for several reasons, one of which is that it impedes the biblical call to continual prayer. But in daily living few give any thought at all to the problem of continual chatter and the account we are to render of it on Judgment Day (Mt 12:36). Most of us have heard over and over in liturgical readings the admonition of Jesus that we must give up all that we possess to be his disciples (Lk 14:33), but few in the humdrum of the day-by-day round even advert to detachment, let alone practice it with any approximation to totality.

So it is with the subject of this chapter. We hear that we are pilgrims, strangers, and nomads on earth (1 Pet 2:11; Heb 11:13–16), and we respond with a ready yes. The Master states plainly that we have no security in anything finite (Lk 12:15), and again we say amen. But when it comes to our routine choices and decisions, most of us act as though we are by no means strangers and nomads here below. We assume that we belong here, that this is our fatherland, that our security is enhanced by a higher salary, a paid-up mortgage, and adequate coverage by insurance. Most people seem to feel so at home in this life that, aside from tragedy that may on occasion cross their paths, they give scarcely a thought to heaven as their real, influencing-me-now goal.

Pilgrims tend to be poor. They choose to have little. By pilgrims here I mean, of course, genuine pilgrims, not those who may use the label as a cover for a pleasure trip. A man traveling with his heart set on the sacred shrine cares little about the hotel or the road or what is or is not in his luggage. Not only does he have little in fact, but also he is completely detached from it in spirit. And he is ready to share spontaneously and generously with fellow pilgrims.

Life itself is a pilgrimage, the supreme journey. We are to be present in this world but not at home in it (SC no. 2). That is the ideal, but unfortunately we have something of the squirrel in us: we are hoarders. We may not be avaricious villains, but we are clingers. We tend to pitch our tent right here and live as though there were no death, no other destiny.

Factual frugality embraced in faith upsets all this illusion. It makes one experientially aware (not simply in abstract theory) that we have here no lasting city. At his last breath the multimillionaire is just as penniless as the dying beggar in a Calcutta street. But few of us are willing to face this plain fact. We prefer illusion because the center of our gravity is not God.

Here emerges the fourth value of faith-filled frugality: it shouts reality into the ears of anyone willing to hear. It dissipates the tinselly illusions of marketing and advertising and consumerism. It declares that elegant dining and drinking, extensive wardrobes, expensive traveling and position, prestige, and pleasure seeking are really side issues, indeed, often impediments, to the main business of life. Few want to hear the declaration, but the poor man and woman proclaim it nonetheless. They are prophetic witnesses to realism.

What I have said thus far in this chapter is upon a few minutes' reflection more than a little obvious. We may turn our attention to an aspect of this witness question that is not so clear, one that is often unrealized. Social thinkers distinguish between operational and ideological structures in the economic life of modern societies. Among the operational structures are monetary systems, tax and tariff laws, trade agreements, welfare and social security systems. Ideological structures are the value assumptions undergirding the operational systems. The former sustain, give life to, and support the latter. If the operational structures are unjust and unloving, they can be changed only if the ideological undergirdings are changed. Ethicists, secular as well as religiously inspired, seem to be of one mind in this matter:

> It can be argued that the single dominating and organizing value in American culture is economic—the good life (an ideological structure). Our American culture promotes and rewards this and thereby educates to it. Even our universities have capitulated to this value. Too often they simply train for the job market. Practically, then, this means that other values will be pursued and promoted only within this overriding priority. Thus, justice in education, housing, medical services, job opportunity is promoted within the dominance of the financial criterion—"if we can afford it", where "afford" refers to the retention of a high level of consumership. The dominance of the economic value is the root of enslavement, the ideological structure.[1]

We may consider a concrete example. At Mass one Sunday morning in October a serious, deeply religious couple

[1] Richard McCormick, *Theological Studies*, Mar., 1973, p. 101; the words in parentheses are added to the original text.

hear that the following week there is going to be a collection for the foreign missions. As they drive home Mrs. Jones is likely to say, "Bill, do you think we could afford something like $20 or $30 for this collection?" After some musing Mr. Jones may well respond that he, too, thinks they could afford that amount as their contribution. While most would indeed consider Mr. and Mrs. Jones a generous couple, we must note something significant. When both of them used the expression "we could afford", they meant "without changing significantly our level of consuming". They did not mean "we could afford $20 or $30 if we dine out less frequently or give up smoking and cocktails, or if we cancel our vacation trip, or sell one of our sports cars." Even in serious people the good life ideology is operative, and it profoundly influences what they do and do not do on the operational level. If Mr. and Mrs. Jones were to give up the good life ideal, they could give far more to the foreign missions.

So it is also on the level of society itself. The gross inequities of our world do not change much despite the deluge of words because the basic premises have not changed. A further thought from our ethicist:

> It is not suggested here that the operational structures do not merit direct and decisive action. They obviously do. But the lasting success of this action is inseparable from modification of the ideological structure. It is precisely here that the prophetic witness of a sparing-sharing use of material goods assumes its importance. This lifestyle is not just good example, alongside of other more practical and direct tasks. It appears to be an essential way of getting at a society's value assumptions, and hence becomes a social ethical responsibility of the first magnitude.[2]

[2] Ibid.

In other words, we need prophetic witnesses. We need people who in their way of life challenge the prevailing false ideologies bearing upon the production, distribution, and use of material goods. We need lived prophecy.

Let me be concrete. The best paid fifth of American white workers earn five or six times more than the worst paid fifth. Those who offer pat solutions to complex problems would probably call on the Congress (or Parliament) to make laws to force greater equity in the distribution of the fruits of production. If a legislative body were to try to establish equity by law, it would have a revolution on its hands. The basic presuppositions of the population must change first. Ideological structures undergird and support laws and other structures.

We therefore need pilgrim witnesses. We need joyous, loving men and women to show in their lives that one can live a sparing-sharing lifestyle and still be happy and fulfilled. We need to induce conversion into the masses first by example, then by word—really, by both simultaneously.

A writer has described a visit he paid to four Little Sisters of Jesus (the congregation inspired by the example and teaching of Charles de Foucauld) in a Muslim slum area of Karachi. When they were asked what the Church needs among these people, the Sisters responded with three suggestions: "First, Christians must be seen to pray. Muslims and Hindus appreciate a life of prayer. They don't see Christians as a prayerful community. Rather they see us running things, like schools. Second, we must be poor. For Asia, true spirituality is inseparable from poverty. Third, we must love the Muslims and be with them in their daily lives." [3] What these Sisters were asking for is poor pilgrim witnesses,

---

[3] Denis Murphy, "A Church in the Minority", *America*, Aug. 25, 1979, p. 76.

witnesses to the fact that God is our center of gravity, not things. They are asking for signs that we have here no lasting city, that we are intent on the fatherland.

Saints are pilgrim witnesses. Saint Columban even as a handsome youth had all the local girls running after him, and yet he deeply felt the transitoriness of things, "the passing of all beauty, including that of women". He was a pilgrim to the bone, and his longing was for the destination, the heavenly homeland. For Columban created splendor was like the grass of the field.[4] He lived what he believed. He was a witness. Saint Hedwig of Poland, daughter of a king, was both deeply loved by her husband and yet held in awe by him because of her holiness. Though she was a faithful wife, she renounced worldly pomp and the glitter of gold and gems. Rather she chose to live a life of asceticism, penance, and prayer. Hedwig died shortly after giving birth to a daughter.[5] Blessed Margaret Clitherow, a married English convert, was a beautiful woman, witty and cheerful. She fasted four days a week and spent an hour and a half in prayer each morning. She died a cheerful martyr in her thirties by being pressed to death for harboring priests and attending Mass.[6] Blessed Anna Maria Taigi, the mother of a large family and a recipient of mystical prayer, was one of the most remarkable and best known women in the nineteenth century. While still young she experienced a love for clothing and a desire to be admired, but this frivolity was followed by conversion. Feminine vanity gave way to pilgrim simplicity.[7]

[4] Daphne Mould, The Irish Saints, p. 107.
[5] Butler, Lives of the Saints, 1:445–46.
[6] Ibid, 1:679–82.
[7] Ibid., 2:513–15.

The most famous poor man after the Lord himself is, of course, Saint Francis of Assisi. Possessing only his habit and his office book, this lovable pilgrim sang his way down the roads of Italy. The liturgy in turn sings of him:

> Scant the measure of his food;
> Scant his raiment, coarse and rude;
> A cord his girdle plain and rude;
> He goes with feet unshod.[8]

Much less known, surely, but perhaps the most striking and unusual illustration of poor pilgrimage is Saint Benedict Joseph Labre. He was literally a tramp, a vagrant, a beggar, an unvarnished pilgrim who wandered from one shrine to another. Benedict was dirty, vermin ridden, weary, hungry, ragged. But he was also a man burning with love for Christ and his penniless brothers and sisters. He was a happy man who sang as he wandered along the road. He chose to be a dire destitute, a man whose shoes "were rotted with holes". Yet this saint was no fool; he knew what he was about: "As a lover is obsessed by the beloved, so Benedict lived continually in the presence of Christ." In continual love and adoration he could wonder about those many people who did not, perhaps could not, understand him.

> What were they getting at—all those sensible, kind, and certainly well-meaning people—when they tried to suggest a cleaner shirt, less down-at-heels shoes, a more conventional hat? Benedict thanked them politely, but in the tone of an artist who is called away from his vision to be told that his tie is undone.[9]

---

[8] Franciscan liturgy, Sequence for feast of Saint Francis.
[9] Agnes de la Gorce, *St. Benedict Joseph Labre*, pp. 90, 93–94.

"Look to the Lord and you will be radiant with joy" (Ps 34:5). But one cannot look to the Lord if he is looking to things. We cannot serve God and mammon. The pilgrim looks to the one, not the other.

PART III

RADICALITY AND SUPERFLUITY

Levels of Radicality

When one looks into the lives of the saints, lay as well as
clerical and religious, he finds that there are varying approaches to the practice of gospel poverty. In saying this I am
not thinking of those who cut corners or dilute the revealed
message. These are not levels of radicality but levels of laxity.

We are concerned with the authentic Gospel and with
those who live it best. We have noted widely diverse examples of how the saints express their approach to material goods.
This variety does not imply contradictory understandings of
Jesus' life and proclamation, but it does imply complementary emphases and practices. The circumstances of some persons call for a more drastic self-denial than those of others.

It may well be also that God calls some to a radicality in
their surrender of created things that goes far beyond that to
which he calls others. There is no doubt that he calls everyone to all of what we describe as level one (though not to
every example we give) and to some of what is included in
level two—at least when one's situation calls for it. A few are
called to level three.

Level One

For the sake of clarity I shall letter the main elements in our
degrees of Gospel poverty. The reader will notice that they

summarize New Testament teaching on the holy use of material creation.

a. *Correct motivation*. Things are means; persons are ends. We misuse things when we use them for their own sakes, that is, as ends. Our sole end in life is immersion in the truth, beauty, joy, celebration, and love that is God. Using finite reality as an end is to make a little god of it. This is why Saint Paul writes that our eating, drinking, and all else are to be done solely for the glory of God, which, of course, is inseparable from our own good (1 Cor 10:31). Though Saint John Fisher's private life was austere (he restricted his sleep to four hours per night, used the discipline, kept a skull before him at mealtime as a reminder of death), he did gather together a fine personal library, said to be among the best in Europe. Yet he formed this collection in view of leaving it to Cambridge University.[1] Saint Elizabeth Ann Seton, while still a widow and responsible for her children, did not give away all her financial resources. She writes to a friend, Julia Scott, that she has a savings account of $500 drawing interest at 5 percent. Yet at the same time Elizabeth writes to Antonio Filicchi that her particular welfare "is always best advanced in poverty and in tears".[2] To be poor in the Gospel sense one must so use things that he can honestly say that the use gives glory to the Father.

b. *Working for one's living*. People who can work but do not are living from the labor of others. So too are those who through laziness do not produce for the benefit of society as they ought. The poor person in the Gospel sense is a man who earns his keep. Saint Paul was explicit: if one does not work, he ought not to eat (2 Thess 3:6–12).

[1] Butler, *Lives of the Saints*, 3:46.
[2] Joseph Dirvin, *Mrs. Seton*, pp. 217, 220.

c. *Sharing to equality* (2 Cor 8:13–15). We have said a great deal about this New Testament requirement, and we need not therefore repeat the message. I may note, however, that though this element is in level one, we ought not to miss its starkness. It is so radical that only the rare person on Earth lives it fully. It is one of those truths whose totality is readily on our lips but seldom in our lives. Gentle, compassionate Saint Robert Bellarmine, himself an archbishop and cardinal, taught that "it is certain that the bishop would sin mortally if, not content with a frugal table and modest furnishings, he fails to spend what money remains on the upkeep of his churches and the sustenance of the poor." [3] If anyone entertains the view that the saint is overly strict on this point, I would suggest he study again 1 John 3:17–18 and James 2:14–17. They who can but do not share with the needy, says John, cannot be loving God, and, according to James, their faith is dead. To lack love and to exist in dead faith are definitions of mortal sin.

d. *Avoidance of superfluities.* If our motivation regarding created reality is correct, it follows that we use only what we need. As Titus 2:12 has it, we are to give up everything that does not lead to God, everything that does not serve a good purpose, everything unneeded. Because we entered the world with nothing and shall leave it with nothing, we are to be content with food and clothing (1 Tim 6:7–8). Robert Bellarmine "would not keep in his possession as trifling a thing as a holy picture or a blessed medal, except the one attached to his rosary beads". When others would try to urge small presents on the saint on the plea that he would then be able to give others small gifts, Robert's answer was that "a poor man ought not to have anything to give away". This scholar

---

[3] James Brodrick, *Robert Bellarmine*, p. 392.

even worried somewhat about keeping in his room his own manuscripts, and he envied the brothers who had no such burdens.[4] Saint Benedict the Black thought it best not to deprive himself of food at table but to eat only a little of what was there.[5] Before his conversion to a wholehearted Gospel life, Saint Francis Borgia was an exceedingly obese man. It did not take him long to conclude that overeating is incompatible with New Testament teaching on superfluities, and slim he became.[6] Saint Vincent de Paul insisted that his Daughters of Charity not seek "dainty treatment" when they were sick, and yet he could add, "but you are not forbidden some little delicacy if you really need it. If one of you is listless and has no appetite for anything, then it is right to give her some dainty; but this must only be done when there is real need for it".[7] In a letter to an archbishop Saint Ignatius Loyola observed that he would not be scandalized if a person brought up in nobility and state were somewhat better dressed and housed even after he has left his state, "considering those that come and go; . . . for it is right to yield to the needs and circumstances of the moment".[8] Saint Mary Michaela Desmaisieres, a Spanish vicountess, solved the problem of necessary banquets, balls, and theatrical performances by wearing under her dress instruments of penance.[9]

e. *Contentment with simplicity.* If one shares to equality and avoids superfluities, his diet, furnishings, clothing, and recreations will be frugal. For 99 percent of the human race elegance is superfluous. The remaining 1 percent for whom

[4] Ibid., p. 65.
[5] Butler, 2:31.
[6] Ibid., 4:76.
[7] Jacques Delarue, *The Holiness of Vincent de Paul*, p. 98.
[8] *Letters and Instructions of St. Ignatius Loyola*, vol. 1, ed. A. Goodier, p. 33.
[9] Butler, 3:405.

some public nobility may be necessary will, if they follow saintly prelates and kings, likewise choose in their private lives to be as frugal as possible. People who have two tunics and give one to the needy neighbor (Lk 3:10–11) are undoubtedly living Gospel simplicity.

f. *Avoidance of vanity.* Deepest personal beauty is found in an inner goodness that radiates outwardly, for if one looks to the Lord, he is radiant with joy (Ps 34:5). The revealed conclusion is clear: do not then imitate the pagans in decking out the body as though external ornaments added anything important. The New Testament twice speaks of exaggerated feminine adornment, and in our day the admonition needs likewise to be addressed to men. Possessing in their baptismal consecration a far greater beauty, Christian women are not to adorn themselves in showy splendor by doing up their hair, wearing elegant clothes and fine jewelry. It is salutary for all of us to realize that primping prettiness is ultimately a losing battle. A woman's imperishable attractiveness rises from her heart, for inner goodness and a sweet disposition are precious to God and to men (1 Pet 3:3–5; cf. also Prov 31:10–31 and 1 Tim 2:9). This inner grace it is that will cause the final splendor of the risen body. Poverty beauty is permanent.

Saints are commonly gentle people, but they are not known for pulling their punches. And they had some choice thoughts about vanity in dress, thoughts we ought to ponder prayerfully. Saint Alphonsus de Liguori observed that "every vain ornament of dress shows that he who wears it is puffed up with vanity", and he cites Saint John Chrysostom to the effect that a "religious who attends to the decoration of her person manifests the deformity of her soul." [10] One may

---

[10] *The True Spouse of Jesus Christ,* c. 9, no. 2.

quarrel with these ideas if he operates on the world's premises, but it is difficult to imagine a plausible argument stemming from Gospel presuppositions.

Level Two

Our levels of poverty interlink and blend into one another. If one lives level one perfectly, he is likely to find himself in level two as well. There are no hard line divisions.

   a. *Giving up necessities for others.* Saint Paul praises the Macedonians, who spontaneously gave from their "intense poverty" to relieve the need of another church, and he notes how they "begged and begged" for this favor of giving, but at the same time the apostle does not require the Corinthians to make extreme sacrifices in their giving (2 Cor 8:1ff.). However, in our modern world of ghastly destitution we may well be called on to surrender lesser necessities to alleviate the sufferings of the billions in dire need. Vatican Council II twice admonished the faithful that it is not enough to give from superfluities but that we are to aid the poor even from our need (GS nos. 69, 88). Pope John Paul II on the occasion of his visit to the United States made the same point. I know of two monasteries in the northern United States in which during the winter months the nuns not merely lower the thermostat; they turn off the heat entirely through the night. In one of the monasteries the heat is also turned off for about four hours during the afternoon. Is there some discomfort? Yes. But as far as I know, no illness follows.

   b. *Begging for the poor and serving them.* Saint Paul begged for his needy ones (2 Cor 8 and 9). So many saints through the centuries have followed his example that I shall not give specific examples. It may suffice for us to note that in this begging and in serving the needy at one's own table the follower of Christ is giving not only what he has but what he is. Because one no longer has possessions to give, he goes out to get the gift and thus gives of his own time and energy—and at the same time reaps the further benefit of ridding himself of some pride.

c. *Poverty just short of destitution.* Through the centuries there have been, and in our day there still are, those persons who wish to live poor with the poor Christ by freely choosing to lack what most people consider the very necessities of life. They live Saint Thomas' principle that "it is good to give your goods to the poor, but it is better to be needy with Christ."[11] Before her conversion Saint Margaret of Cortona lived in public sin as the mistress of a wealthy young cavalier. After his death she had a change of heart, did public penance, and while still a laywoman lived on alms, gave herself to prayer and the care of the poor. Any "unbroken food" she received she gave away; what was left of the broken food she used for herself and for her child born out of wedlock. As Margaret grew older she slept at night on the bare ground, and her diet consisted of a little bread and raw vegetables. Water was her drink. Her generosity and poverty and penance were rewarded with the gift of ecstatic prayer. She died at the age of fifty after living twenty-nine years in penance.[12] Saint Clare and her nuns wore nothing on their feet, slept on the ground, and kept perpetual abstinence. Clare went beyond the penances of the rule by always wearing a hairshirt and during Lent eating nothing but bread and water. Some days she ate nothing at all. Later her bishop and Saint Francis himself prevailed upon her to mitigate her austerities a little, but she

---

[11] II-II, q. 32, a. 8.
[12] Butler, 1:396–99.

never lost her extraordinary love for the Cross.[13] A contemporary of St. Bruno described the poverty of the Carthusians in these words: "Their dress is poorer than that of other monks; so short and thin and rough that the very sight frightens one. They wear hair shirts next their skin and fast almost perpetually; eat only bran-bread; never touch flesh, either sick or well; never buy fish, but eat it if given them as an alms."[14] In her desire to share the insecurity of Christ, Saint Teresa of Avila remarked that "it is a great pleasure for us to find ourselves in a house from which we may at any time be turned out, when we remember that the Lord of the world had no house at all."[15] Though she wanted her monasteries to be conducive to health and prayer, she also wished "everything left rough and unpolished".[16] As to her own person, the foundress observed that "it is when I possess least that I have the fewest worries, and the Lord knows that, as far as I can tell, I am more afflicted when there is excess of anything than when there is lack of it."[17]

Level Three

One who has persevered thus far in this discussion of levels of radicality may understandably wonder how anyone of sound mind would think of going further than what we have just considered. But some have gone further, and in our effort to grasp their lives and message we may not forget the divine

[13] Ibid., 3:309–13.
[14] Ibid., 4:42.
[15] *Foundations*, c. 19.
[16] *Life*, c. 33, no. 12.
[17] *Way of Perfection*, c. 2.

proclamation, "My thoughts are not your thoughts, and my ways are not your ways." These people have put on the divine mind, and they are vividly aware that they are mere nomads on the face of the earth, nomads who have their eyes and hearts fixed on the homeland and on nothing else.

Level three is the level of destitution, a level that is not required by the Gospel but nonetheless is highly praised in those to whom this radical gift is given. The poor widow gave "all she had to live on" to the temple treasury, and she is therefore highly commended by Jesus (Mk 12:41–44). Saint Paul writes glowingly of the Macedonians, who gave to a needy church from their "intense poverty" and "far more than they could afford" (2 Cor 8:1–4). Though it may be going too far to say that Jesus lived a life of destitution during his apostolic years, yet he did choose to have no place to lay his head (Mt 8:20) and to die literally possessionless on the Cross.

Many are the saints who felt the call and received the grace to embrace a life of destitution out of love for the destitute themselves and for the sake of the kingdom. Saint Ephraem lived on barley bread and vegetables and wore a gown that was "all patches".[18] Saint Macrina, who belonged to a family of saints,[19] upon the death of her mother disposed of the estate in behalf of the poor, lived by the work of her hands, and slept on two boards. She died so poor that her brother Gregory had to secure a linen robe so she would have something appropriate for burial.[20] Saint Peter of Alcantara so restricted his diet that he is said to have lost the sense of

[18] Butler, 2:574–75.
[19] Saints Basil the Elder and Emmelia were her parents and Saints Basil the Great, Peter of Sebastea, and Gregory of Nyssa were brothers.
[20] Butler, 3:145.

taste, "for when vinegar and salt was [sic] thrown into a por-
ringer of warm water, he took it for his usual bean soup".
He usually slept once in three days and used the floor as his
bed. He had only one habit, so that when it was being washed
or mended he went into seclusion until it was dry or re-
paired.[21] Saint John Kanti likewise slept on the floor and
never ate meat.[22] Saint Benedict Joseph Labre dined on one
meal a day, "eating only bits of toast soaked in water and
vegetables, particularly peas. On Sundays he submitted to
having two meals, which we even seasoned with a pinch of
salt, and having a few dry nuts as dessert."[23]

Saint Catherine of Siena was rather in a class by herself.
She dieted in an extraordinary manner not to be imitated by
ordinary mortals: no food. Raymond of Capua, her confes-
sor, wrote that "not only did she have no need of food but
she could not in fact take any without it causing her pain."
He adds that "she went without food or drink for the whole
of Lent until the feast of our Lord's Ascension; and yet despite this she was always bursting with life and happiness."
She finally ate on Ascension Day, but "when that day was
over, she resumed her habitual fasting. Then she gradually
reached a state of total abstinence." She likewise forced herself (and admitted its difficulty) to "learn to do without sleep"
and so came to the point where she needed only one-half
hour every other day.[24]

In his household Cardinal Saint Robert Bellarmine saw to
it that during the winter large fires burned in the hall and
the kitchen lest others be cold, but for himself the saint would

---

[21] Butler, 4:144–48.
[22] Ibid., 4:154.
[23] Agnes de la Gorce, *St. Benedict Joseph Labre*, p. 114.
[24] Raymond of Capua, *The Life of St. Catherine of Siena*, pp. 154–56 and 54.

have nothing from one end of the winter to the other. If a guest came, he would light a fire beforehand, but as soon as the visitor left, out would go the fire too.[25]

With a somewhat agitated conscience the reader may well be wondering at this point to what level of poverty God is calling him. Happily I may excuse myself from providing the answer. Writing a book is not the same task as giving individualized spiritual direction. Each of us is to ponder the content of the Gospel in prayer and with the guidance of an enlightened and holy director come to the decision regarding particulars. Our examination of conscience in Chapter 16 may be helpful in this discerning process.

[25] James Brodrick, *Robert Bellarmine*, p. 170.

I I

Necessities and Superfluities

In his book *The Affluent Society*, John Kenneth Galbraith remarks that "what is called a high standard of living consists, in considerable measure, in arrangements for avoiding muscular energy, for increasing sensual pleasure and enhancing caloric intake above any conceivable nutritional requirement." While few will contest the validity of this statement, few are those living in an affluent society who can avoid falling under its censure.

Until we are converted by the Gospel, and completely converted, we tend in dozens of ways to seek what we do not need. Most people most of the time indulge in superfluities without the least awareness of it. How often do we eat and drink what we do not need? Indeed, we eat and drink and inhale over and over again what medical people tell us is detrimental to our health. How often do we rest when we are not weary? Speak when there is utterly no need for it? Buy clothing when we have not worn out what is in the closet (and some will bristle at this suggestion that they should wear out their clothes)? Secure appliances that prevent us from getting the exercise our bodies need for their well-being? Ride when it would be better for us to walk?

How may we define a superfluity? Most people, I think, would agree that anything—words, food, rest, explanation, motion—is superfluous when it is not needed. No problem here.

But this does not settle the matter decisively, for we are led into the next question: And what is needed? Most would agree in the abstract that a luxury is not a necessity, but in the concrete many disagree, violently at times, as to which is which. One man considers a color television set a luxury, while another assumes it to be a necessity in modern life. One woman thinks thirty-five outfits in her closets are necessary for her station in life, while another looks upon such a wardrobe as extravagance. So it goes in matters of travel, vacations, recreation (time, amount, type), pursuit of culture, personal library, appliances and conveniences, heating and air conditioning, hobbies and amusements, dining and drinking, talking and reading.

Our problem, then, is basically to determine what is a necessity. And this question cannot be answered except in terms of finality, purpose, goal. There are therefore two kinds of necessity from this point of view: ends and means. Ends are sought for themselves because they are good in and for themselves. Knowing and loving are such. This is why God is the supreme necessity. He is pure love and truth and delight, the final end or purpose of the human person. He is absolutely necessary not only for himself and in himself (he could not not be) but also for us. Without him we are eternally frustrated, and that is hell. We may call ends like knowing and loving intrinsic necessities. From their very nature we must have them in and for themselves. Absolutely no reason justifies our being without them.

Means are not necessary in themselves, but only when we must have them to get us to indispensable ends or purposes. Teaching is necessary because in our human situation a child cannot mature to his full potential without education at home or in a school. Instruction is necessary as a means to something else. Food and drink are needed as means to health, an end.

A superfluity therefore is a thing that is needed neither for itself as an end nor as a means to get to something that is so needed. Food is superfluous when because of quality and/or quantity it is not needed for health. The weight charts bear out concretely what I am saying here philosophically. Indeed, excessive caloric intake positively damages health. Only a hedonistic individual maintains that eating and drinking are ends in themselves. Even most animals avoid this mistake.

We cannot consequently answer the question of superfluity except in terms of the final destiny of man. This destiny we learn from God: a final enthralling transformation in him through an eternal embrace of vision, love, and delight. This is the supreme necessity. Those conditions and activities are indispensable which lead us to this final enthrallment, which enthrallment is also God's glorification in us. Those conditions and activities are superfluous and therefore positively damaging (at least as hindering progress, if not blocking it out) that do not lead to him. This is the advice given to Titus: we must give up everything that does not lead to God (Tit 2:12).

Pursuing a superfluity is pursuing a dead end. We humans by the original fall are wounded in many ways, and one of them is that we constantly transform means into ends. We do not use food and drink as means to get us to our final goal. We make them into little gods as though we were nothing but combinations of taste buds and stomach. We want clothing not simply to keep warm and to preserve modesty but to show off a beauty that we may not have (it is often the dress that is beautiful, not the body that is in it). In any event wardrobes are expanded because clothes become ends, as though we were made to live in the minds of others: "Won't they think I am gorgeous when they see me in this stunning outfit?" We desire travel and television not simply as aids to our genuine destiny. We transform them into the destiny itself, as though we were made for nothing but new sights and new excitements.

We have here perhaps the most radical reason why people differ so much in their opinions about what is necessary and what is superfluous, what is luxury and what is not. We differ in our life goals. If I have chosen pleasure and prestige as my overriding goals in life, I am going to differ immensely from you, who are profoundly convinced that immersion in God is your top priority. Saints were and are of one mind as to what is superfluous because they were and are of one mind about goals.

If my center of gravity is in this world, my concepts of necessity and superfluity will derive from this orientation. Prestige will be important to me, and I will consider indispensable an extensive wardrobe and an impressive home. Pleasure will loom large, and I will take it for granted that I have a right to a long, costly vacation, or perhaps several of them, each year. Gourmet dining and drinking will appear normal to me and part of "what I need" to make it in our pressurized world. Sexual pleasure will be something sought for its own sake, and so naturally I reject any moral teaching that suggests otherwise. Self-denial and penance and mortification seem foreign to my mind, and really I see very little need for them in my life, for after all, my style of life "doesn't hurt anyone". When I prosper with good things, I am like the man in the Gospel with the bursting barns, who thinks not at all of sharing his wealth with the poverty striken. Rather he builds larger barns to hold his wealth. He says to himself, "Eat, drink, and be merry, for you have lots in store for years to come."

If on the other hand my center of gravity is in the bosom of the Trinity, my concepts of necessity and superfluity will be drastically different. Prestige will not matter, nor elegant clothing, not delicate dining and drinking, nor sensual pleasure. Necessity will require that I see means as means and not as ends, that I desire and use only what contributes to my final destiny and to the glory of the God I love above all else. I will live sparingly so that I may share with my needy sisters and brothers.

To push our inquiry further, we may now consider those for whom God is everything. They agree about necessity and superfluity because they agree about the goal, not simply with an intellectual agreement, but with a real one that concretizes itself in everyday choices. These people realize that there are different types of necessity, and that therefore there is a valid sense in which what is necessary for one person may not be such for another. There are some things, of course, that are absolutely indispensable for everyone. We may then distinguish four kinds of necessity:

1 *Survival needs.* No one can live long without food, drink, and shelter. And no one questions that these are indeed necessities.

2 *Health needs.* Men are not merely to survive; they are to maintain a reasonable level of well-being. Under this caption we would place proper diet, clean air and water, adequate recreation, exercise, and rest. Once again, almost no one would refuse to accept these as genuine necessities even if they are of a less pressing type.

3 *Spiritual needs.* Because we are not merely biological entities, we have needs that soar beyond the material order and find their ultimate fulfillment only in the bosom of Father,

Son, and Spirit. We must have, therefore, individual and communal prayer, a suitable place and adequate times for worship, formal instruction, and personal guidance. We need books and candles and bread and wine. We need an institutional Church to teach, govern, sanctify—a Church that will preserve us from our subjective meanderings and illusions.

4 *Functional needs*. Because we are men, not angels, we have work to do in our world, and in complicated modern society work cannot be done without means. For my work I need a laptop or typewriter and I need jets. Without the one I could not readily handle correspondence; without the other I would have to cancel perhaps one-third of my engagements. While these functional needs are neither survival nor health needs, they are important.

In our assessment of what we mean by necessity/superfluity and what we intend to do about them in our lives, we may not bypass the question of degrees and types of need in relation to our neighbor. If a brother or sister is literally starving for sheer lack of nourishment, I must be willing to give up my less pressing needs if by so doing I can alleviate his dire lack. This is why both Vatican Council II and Pope John Paul II have called on wealthy societies to come to the aid of the poor, not only from their superfluities but also from their need. I may illustrate this from a brief notice in one of our daily newspapers:

> Jean Mayer, the Harvard nutritionist, urged Americans today to limit themselves to one drink at parties as a way of increasing the grain supply to underfed countries.
>
> Most alcohol is made from grain, and Dr. Mayer said that Americans drink enough beer and cocktails each year to feed 40 million to 50 million people.

"I'm not preaching prohibition," Dr. Mayer said, "I'm just preaching moderation. It would be better for our health, it would be better for our pocketbooks and it would be better for our consciences." [1]

Many of our contemporaries would insist that they need their wine and cocktails as a mode of relaxation. Whether this contention can be supported by evidence may be subject to debate, but in any event lesser needs must cede to the greater. It is difficult to see how a reasonable person could debate that.

Even though most of us know better in our reflective moments, we commonly suppose that abounding luxury begets happiness and voluntary poverty gives rise to a bleak, dull existence. We address this question more fully in our chapter on joy, and yet it may be useful to indicate here the liabilities attendant on indulging in superfluities. Just as every sin carries within itself its own punishment in this life as well as in the next (unless atoned for), so also every unneeded indulgence comes fitted with its bag of miseries.

Focusing on things, turning means into ends, dulls the mind. To the extent that a person loves finite reality for itself and aside from God, a sinful aberration, he is blinded to divine truth. There are degrees of dullness, of course, but experience makes it plain that as people are more or less immersed in the world they are more or less obtuse regarding God. We cannot serve both God and mammon. The more worldly people are blinded, the less they know it. They are in a condition worse than that of the man born blind. He at least knows that he does not know color. This worldling may read Scripture and the saints, but he never grasps the message in more than an arid, verbal way. Most likely he will be sure that "that is all nonsense". Saint Paul al-

---

1. *New York Times*, November 9, 1974, p. 6.

ready anticipated this spiritual dwarf when he told the Corinthians that the worldly man cannot understand the things of the Spirit—not simply does not, but cannot understand (1 Cor 2:14). Or as Jesus himself put it: Though the light has come into the world, men show they prefer darkness because of their evil deeds (Jn 3:19). The person who uses things as they are meant to be used, that is, as means to God, is real. And the more real one is, the more one sees reality and the Author of reality.

The second liability attendant on indulging in superfluities is a loss of taste for prayer. It is ironic how people facilely speak of the absence of God and fail to see that it is they who have absented themselves from him. God is always present to anyone who wants him. He may be present at times in dark purification, but he is present nonetheless. God never absents himself. As a banner I recently saw put it, "If God is absent, guess who moved." It is not accidental that those who indulge in unneeded travel, recreation, dining, clothing are never much given to prayer. Once again, we cannot serve God and mammon. We choose one or the other; we cannot have both. Strange it is that when people experience emptiness in prayer, they assume the main problem must be that they have not yet found the right book or the right technique—oriental or occidental. Scripture says nothing about method at prayer, but it does say a great deal about true poverty. The main problem in developing a deep prayer life is by far the failure to live the radicality of the Gospel, hour by hour and day by day.

The third harm focuses on our neighbor. If I welcome superfluities in my life, I am depriving my brother of what is his, as both Saint Ambrose and Pope Paul VI have reminded us. We read in 1 John 3:17–18 that if a man has good things and does not share with the needy neighbor, he cannot be loving God. Or as Saint John the Baptist bluntly told his listeners, if you have two tunics, and your neighbor has none, give him one. One may profitably wonder what the Baptist would have said of the man or woman with dozens of outfits in the closet? I hear thunder on the horizon.

The fourth harm: one who seeks what he does not need is devoid of the pure delight God reserves for those who seek him undividedly. If the reader has the least doubt about this, I urge him to believe the mystics. I urge him to read and ponder prayerfully the complete works of Saint John of the Cross, for he will find that the pleasures of Earth pale next to those God lavishly pours into those who are entirely purified of all self-seeking. I ask the doubter to believe Saint Paul when he says that eye has not seen nor ear heard, nor can our wildest imagination suspect, what God has prepared even in this life for those who love him (1 Cor 2:9). I ask him to believe Jesus himself when he promises immeasurably more, the hundredfold, also in this life, to those who surrender everything the world values to follow him (Lk 18:29–30).

The fifth liability burdening the pursuer of superfluity is a host of inner disturbances: "what do they think of me? . . . How does my hair look? . . . is my figure trim; is my skin smooth and unspotted? . . . Are our visitors impressed by these drapes . . . or our car . . . or this rug . . . or our collection of books and periodicals . . . or a hundred other things? . . . What if I am deprived of this nibbling or this snack? . . . Perhaps I will not get to the television first and get the program I want . . . the type of salad dressing I like is not on the table . . . my rosary is not as striking as his . . . this room is not as warm as I would like it to be . . . I did not get a copy of that new holy picture . . . I am so bored; I wish there were someone I could talk to . . . what a dull, empty evening . . ." The pursuer of superfluity quite completely lacks the fulfilling joy and the rest that Jesus promises to the burdened who come to him (Mt 11:28–30).

The final harm I shall mention is that one who seeks created things beyond what he needs will not attain mystical love. He is unable to grow to the point where he tastes and sees how good the Lord is (Ps 34:5); his heart and his flesh will never sing for joy in the living God (Ps 84:2). He will not experience what Vatican Council II spoke of as normal for all the faithful of all vocations, namely, that they taste to their full of the paschal mysteries and be set on fire within the eucharistic celebration (SC no. 10). Religious who fail to observe their vow of poverty will not be "thoroughly enriched with the treasures of mysticism" that should be found in those who labor in spreading the Gospel (AG no. 18).

If the reader wishes to pursue this question of the harm done by superfluities and what to do about the problem, I can refer him to no better source than Saint John of the Cross' *Ascent of Mount Carmel*. It is the classic on the problem of inordinate desires and their active purification.

Some people, I suspect, have difficulty in pinpointing what is and what is not superfluous in their lives. Consultation with an informed and prayerful spiritual director can often be immensely helpful, but to some extent each person must make his own decisions. Needs vary, and because we cannot get into another's skin, we cannot know in every case whether a need is real or illusory. It may be useful, therefore, to suggest here an examen, a kind of checklist of pertinent questions. With their help and in a prayerful setting each of us should be able to determine his own answers.

1. By what standards do I determine what is necessary?
2. Do I collect unneeded things? Do I hoard possessions?
3. May I, on Gospel principles, buy clothes at the dictates of fashion designers in Paris and New York? Am I slave to fashion? Do I live in other peoples' minds?

Why really do I have all the clothes I have: shirts, blouses, suits, dresses, shoes, gloves?

4. Am I an inveterate nibbler? Do I eat because I am bored? Do the weight charts convict me of superfluity in eating and drinking? Do I take second helpings simply for the pleasure they afford?
5. Do I keep unneeded books and papers and periodicals and notes?
6. Do I retain two or three identical items (clocks, watches, scarves) of which I really need only one?
7. Do I spend money on trinkets and unnecessary conveniences?
8. In the winter, do we keep our thermostat at a setting higher than health experts advise: 68 degrees?
9. When I think of my needs, do I also think of the far more drastic needs of the teeming millions in the third world?
10. Do I need the traveling I do more than the poor need food and clothing and medical care?
11. Am I right in contributing to the billions of dollars spent each year on cosmetics? How much of this can be called necessary?
12. Is smoking necessary for me?
13. Is drinking necessary for me?
14. Do I need to examine exactly what I mean by saying to myself, "I need this"?
15. Can I honestly say that all I use or possess is used or possessed for the glory of God (1 Cor 10:31)? Would he be given more glory by some other use?
16. Do I in the pauline sense "mind the things above, not those on earth" (Col 3:1–2)?

PART IV

STATES IN LIFE

12

Frugality in Marriage

Not everyone begins a book at the beginning, which as *The Sound of Music* has it, is a very good place to begin. Because there are probably other good places to begin in some human enterprises, I would not be surprised if some of my partners in this dialogue have selected the present chapter as their jump-off point. And *jump-off* may have two meanings here.

In any event I would imagine that, wherever they begin, laymen who pick up this book with serious intent do so with some apprehension. If that concern were verbalized, it might go something like the following: "In my years of listening to Sunday sermons I do not recall a single instance in which the preacher presented any kind of poverty as an ideal in marriage. Usually the poor are people to be helped with money and gifts. Occasionally I have heard of the vow of poverty religious take, and even that I by no means understand. So what in the world could a book like this one say in a realistic manner to me, a married person? Is it anything more than the author's private opinions? Is he mixing up vocations?"

Those who began this book at the beginning will not be surprised to be reminded that Scripture scholars are quite agreed that almost everything the New Testament says about a sparing-sharing way of life is said for everyone in every vocation. We have already admitted, indeed, have stated plainly, that this is the most radical teaching on the use of material goods known to mankind. We have begun with the confusions and problems and difficulties most people in all vocations have about this subject. In solving these problems, we began with premises and principles and have slowly seen the rare beauty of the divine message. It would therefore seem to me important that anyone—cleric, lay, religious—begin this study at the literal beginning. Everything thus far is said for everyone, and what follows in these vocation chapters must suppose all that precedes. Specialized calls to Gospel poverty just cannot be understood aside from the general call addressed to all. What then remains to be added in this chapter? What is special for married men and women?

The main message at this point is that the ideal is real. Though the message is simple, it is by no means easy for most people to accept, let alone live. It is safe to say that the typical man on the street scarcely ever gives a thought to the idea that frugal living is a religious ideal. Never does he view it as somehow obligatory. To this person's mind, if there is such an ideal and/or obligation, it is the concern of monks and nuns alone. Period.

How do we establish that the ideal is real . . . real for the wedded as for everyone else? My favorite way is the saints, in this case the married saints. Without exception they combined a care for their family with a bountiful sharing with the needy. Without exception they were beautifully fulfilled and happy people. They are proofs in the flesh that Jesus' teaching works in practical life.

I do not say that they had no problems in living the Gospel in their lay life. Nor do I suggest that they lacked critics. They, like the rest of us, had their share of both. Critics after all are often signs of the target's authenticity, for those who live faithfully in Christ Jesus are sure to be attacked (2 Tim 3:12). God's thoughts are not ours, and many people do not like them.

Our suggestions for frugality in lay life may be summarized according to several captions:

1. Value motivation
2. Maintaining one's state
3. Secular signs
4. Challenging the world
5. Focusing on beauty
6. Saintly radicality

Even though the concrete situations of married men and women vary widely, and those too of single persons, yet there are characteristics common to all.

1. *Value motivation.* Because strictly speaking poverty is a negative situation, we do not seek it for itself. We pursue it for the positive values for which it prepares us, the values it makes possible. In Chapters 6 through 9 we considered these values: radical readiness for the divine word . . . a sparing lifestyle making sharing possible . . . apostolic credibility . . . pilgrim witness. I wish here simply to remind the layperson that in thinking about how he shall concretize the Gospel message, he may not forget these four values. They pertain to him as they pertain to the priest and the religious.

2. *Maintaining one's state.* A modest research into the lives of the lay saints leads me to conclude that at least generally if not unanimously they did not push poverty to the point of neglecting their position in life. Saint Thomas More, a married man and a father, while living a simple life himself, saw to it that his children had what would further their educational development. He was careless of personal appearance, and he preferred staples to delicacies in his diet. He drank

small beer or water, "merely touching wine with his lips, as a matter of courtesy". He dressed simply, "never wearing his gold chain, if he can help it"—Thomas was chancellor of England under Henry VIII. Yet for the sake of his children and perhaps his own delight he kept several rare animals: ape, fox, beaver, weasel. Of the saint we read that "anything from abroad, or otherwise remarkable, he buys at once. His house is full of noteworthy things, and he loves to see others pleased with them." [1] This is the husband and father in whose family circle evening prayer was daily said, and Scripture reading and discussion were part of ordinary meals. To his table the poor rather than the rich were invited. Thomas himself rose at two in the morning for prayer and study, and he participated in daily Mass. The saint corresponded with his children in Latin rather than in the vernacular, presumably to further their literary skills.

Austere Elizabeth of Hungary loved her husband dearly, enjoyed being with him, shared his life intimately, prayed with him, rushed to meet him on his return from a journey "covering his mouth with a thousand kisses." [2] She wore beautiful clothes when it pleased him, but he seemed not to know that under her dress his wife habitually also wore a hairshirt. [3] While still a radiant bride in her early twenties Elizabeth was lavish in her largess toward the poor and in her caring tenderly for them with her own hands despite their repulsive sores and dirt. We are told that she had "an implacable impulse to poverty which in her was a divine vocation". [4]

[1] R. W. Chambers, *Thomas More*, p. 176.
[2] Nesta de Robeck, *Saint Elizabeth of Hungary*, pp. 48–49.
[3] Ibid., p. 49.
[4] Ibid., p. 100.

In his direction of Saint Jane Frances de Chantal while she was still a young widowed mother, Saint Francis de Sales limited her mortifications with the reminder that she was still a woman in the world. Yet at the same time he was not reluctant to ask once upon seeing her dressed better than usual, "Madam, do you wish to marry again?" Upon hearing her negative answer, he added, "Very well, but then you should pull down your flag." [5]

Charles de Foucauld offered a simple norm for lay frugality in a letter to his married sister: "Yes, live simply, avoid any unnecessary expense; in your manner and way of life, withdraw ever further from everything that smacks of the world, vanity, and pride. . . . There must be no economizing on good books (spiritual masters and lives of the saints) . . . no economizing on alms; no reductions here, but rather increases. . . . Trust, trust! Be free from all anxiety. . . . God will arrange [your children's] future a hundred thousand times better than you and all the people in the world put together could do." [6]

3. *Secular signs.* Medical doctors are agreed that if we in wealthy, technological societies ate and exercised as good health requires, we would be a long way toward living frugally. One secular source observed that "if the 110 million adult Americans who are overweight—by 2.3 *billion* pounds—were all put on a diet to achieve proper weight, say two University of Illinois (Urbana) scientists, the nation would save almost six trillion calories. . . . And that's just for the first year. If they all stayed on their diets, the nation would save more than three trillion calories each and every year thereafter." [7] In another study on the aging process we are told that

[5] Butler, *Lives of the Saints*, 3:370.
[6] J. F. Six, *Spiritual Autobiography of Charles de Foucauld*, pp. 125–26.
[7] James K. Page, *Reader's Digest*, June 1979, p. 9.

if you can control your eating, you can significantly control your aging as well, say the experts. You not only are what you eat—you *age* by what you eat!—Less overeating has definitely proven helpful. Starved rats outlived their fattened cousins in a laboratory experiment, almost doubling the normal life-span. And, they refused to grow transplanted malignant tumors, while the well-stuffed rats nurtured the transplants and died. Dr. Edward Bortz, past-president of the American Medical Association and the American Geriatrics Society maintains that we would be better off if our food intake were about half what the average American consumes today.[8]

4. *Challenging the world.* The lay vocation is a secular, in-the-world way of life. Like leaven in the mass, the layman is to penetrate the world with the spirit and life of the Gospel. Because God's thoughts are far removed from ours (Is 55:8–9), the deeply converted layman is radically different from the large majority of his counterparts. He is a challenge in the flesh. Not that he preaches daily homilies in shop or office. But he must be different—and not all will like the difference. Though he is living in this world, his center of gravity is not on earth; it is in the bosom of the Trinity. He is a pilgrim, a stranger, a nomad plodding along to the fatherland (1 Pet 2:11; Heb 11:13–16).

We may illustrate with the divine word. The same first letter of Peter that just told us we are pilgrims goes on to tell Christian women that they should not be concerned about dressing up for show, spending time on doing up their hair, wearing gold bracelets and fine dresses. Their beauty should stem from an inner radiance of goodness, the "ornament of a sweet and gentle disposition" (1 Pet 3:3–5). There are few

---

[8] *Braniff Place*, Jan. 1975, p. 26.

women willing to allow their own simple feminine goodness proclaim their person beauty. Most feel the need of ar-
tificial props in cosmetics and clothing and jewelry—and
increasingly so do men.

Saint Elizabeth of Hungary, destined as she was for marriage, already as a young girl was captured by Christ. At the
age of ten or eleven she publicly challenged the world's values
when in a packed church she removed her crown and pros-
trated herself before the crucifix. When called to order for this
most unconventional deed, Elizabeth responded, "How can
I, a miserable creature, remain wearing a crown of earthly dig-
nity when I see my King Jesus Christ crowned with thorns?" [9]
How many of us take all this seriously? How many closets
are jammed with dozens of dresses and suits and coats because the world dictates that one just must wear a different
outfit each day? Does hygiene really require that outer clothing be changed every day? Or does "I want to be neat and
clean" really translate into "I want to be admired, thought to
be beautiful. What people think of me is terribly important
to me, for I am living in their minds"?

Saint Vincent Ferrer was famous for his miracles. With a
touch of humor one of his biographers wrote after the saint
managed to persuade some elegant ladies to modify their
fantastic headdresses that this was "the greatest of all his marvelous deeds".[10] Indeed, it may have been.

Down deep we all know that clothing and jewelry are not
the person. The individual in elegant evening dress is not
one atom different from the same person in paint-smeared
work clothes. The Christian is immeasurably more interested in the splendor of truth, the symphony of music, the

beauty of nature and art, the glory of prayer and selfless human love. These are values no thief can reach, no moth destroy (Lk 12:33).

5. *Focusing on beauty*. Laymen can do the Church and the world an immense favor if in their lives they replace consumerism with a concern for genuine beauty and so form their children. Long before it was fashionable (1535) Saint Thomas More saw to it that his three daughters received an education on a par with that of his son. To one of their tutors, William Gonell, the saint wrote while away at court that his children should be taught "not to be dazzled at the sight of gold; not to lament that they do not possess what they erroneously admire in others; not to think more of themselves for gaudy trappings, nor less for the want of them; neither to deform the beauty that nature has given them by neglect, nor to try to heighten it by artifice; to put virtue in the first place, learning in the second".[11] Then, advising Gonell to introduce his children to the writings of Saints Jerome and Augustine, Thomas continues, "Thus peace and calm will abide in their hearts, and they will be disturbed neither by fulsome flattery nor by the stupidity of those illiterate men who despise learning. . . . And thus you will bring about that my children, who are dear to me by nature, and still more dear by learning and virtue, will become most dear by that advance in knowledge and good conduct."[12]

6. *Saintly radicality*. Were we to bring this chapter to a halt at this point, we probably would please more people than we will by continuing on with still greater radicality. But the whole truth must be told: some lay and married saints went

[11] E. E. Reynolds, *St. Thomas More* (New York: Doubleday Image edition), p. 111.
[12] Ibid.

still further. If the Church has seen fit to canonize them as examples of heroic Gospel living, who are we to be scandalized by their heroicity?

With her husband's approval Saint Frances of Rome lived for long years on bread and vegetables and at the same time begged for the poor. Though she was most careful of her duties as wife and mother, Frances wore plain dresses and eventually sold all her jewelry. Lorenzo, her husband, knew he was living with a saint, and he seemed to have placed no obstacles to his wife's unconventional way of life.[13]

Saint Margaret of Scotland, wife, queen, and mother of eight, kept two lents, one before Easter, the other before Christmas. During these seasons she (often with her husband) rose at midnight for matins. Margaret cared for the poor and fed them daily with her own hands. She ate sparingly and permitted herself little sleep so she would have more time for prayer.[14]

As a hardworking layman, judge, soldier, husband, Saint Nicholas von Flue fasted four days a week (and the whole of lent, of course) on a daily piece of bread or a few dried pears. His health did not suffer, nor did his long hours of contemplative prayer. Later, as a hermit, Nicholas ate nothing for years on end. Agents of the civil government for an entire month kept strict watch to make sure he received no food. The local bishop tested the saint once by asking him what virtue was most meritorious. "When he replied obedience, he was bidden to eat a sop of bread soaked in blessed wine. He obeyed, but at the cost of such agonies that he was never again asked to eat anything."[15]

---

[13] Butler, 1:529–33.
[14] Butler, 2:516.
[15] E. I. Watkin, "St. Nicholas von Flue", in *Saints and Ourselves*, ed. P. Caraman (New York: Doubleday Image edition), pp. 159, 165.

Saint Hedwig, a married woman, wore a hairshirt and the same tunic and cloak winter and summer. She walked to church barefooted over ice and snow, and carried her shoes for possible use in case she met anyone on the way.[16]

While still a teenager Saint Aloysius rose at midnight for prayer, took the discipline, and fasted three times a week on bread and water.[17] As a young single woman Saint Catherine of Siena lived in a small room of her parents' home a life of prayer and fasting. She took the discipline and slept on boards.[18] Likewise as a laywoman Saint Angela Merici already lived an austere life in which her diet was almost entirely bread, vegetables, and water.[19]

As a young layman Saint Philip Neri ate "a roll of bread daily. This he munched with a handful of olives for meat, washing the repast down with a cup of water drawn from the well. It was as a rule his sole meal. Often he ate nothing at all, sometimes going without food three days in succession."[20] This seems to have been Philip's way of life for seventeen years before he was ordained a priest. As a young layman we hear of him "reading on the porches of churches in the moonlight, because he was too poor to be able to afford a candle to light his pages. . . . In this way he studied for two years."[21]

The reader will not conclude that each of the above examples is presented as a practice that must be followed by anyone worthy of the Gospel. Yet at the same time we have

[16] Butler, 4:124.
[17] Ibid., 2:605.
[18] Ibid., 2:193.
[19] Ibid., 2:432.
[20] Theodore Maynard, *Mystic in Motley: The Life of St. Philip Neri* (Milwaukee: Bruce Publishing, 1946), p. 25.
[21] Ibid., p. 29.

no warrant to evade or ignore what these heroes and heroines teach about the use of material goods and our final destiny. It may be worth noting that laypeople may derive further insights into the practice of frugality from the following chapters directed to clerics and religious, just as the latter may benefit greatly from the example of lay saints. While the three vocations are not identical, people living them can surely learn from one another. Sanctity is one, even though the means are partially diverse.

13

The Religious Vow

If we may in a sense term religious the professional poor, that is, those who have made a life profession of living in a special, radical way the gospel message dealing with the use of material things, then we may also say that the professionals are perplexed. A great deal of this perplexity we have considered in Chapter 2. This evangelical counsel is so wide in its scope, so rich in its history that I do not in a single chapter intend even to touch on all that could be said about it. Moreover, almost everything in this book is obviously relevant to people who publicly assert by vow that they are going to follow the poor Christ. What we shall do in these few pages is discuss questions that are particularly pertinent to religious congregations:

1. Virginity/celibacy calls for frugality.
2. Freedom from compensation compromises.
3. The ecclesial dimension of the vow.
4. Has the religious vow of poverty changed in its meaning?
5. The common life.
6. Why is there so much inertia in practice?

We shall suppose here what is taught both in the documents of Vatican Council II and in all subsequent magisterial statements dealing with religious life.

1. *Virginity calls for frugality.* The innocent word *calls* in our caption is to be understood in a strong sense. It is equivalent in our meaning to *demands.* Our point is not merely that in the New Testament and in the nature of things the two vows of chastity and poverty are as a matter of fact juxtaposed in a certain way of life. Two bricks in a wall are juxtaposed, but one brick does not of its nature demand the other (although the wall does). The point is that the one vow requires the other as its indispensable complement. I shall show this in five ways.

First, revelation itself. The New Testament links humility, continence, and poverty together as specially related to the kingdom, to what Jesus is about in his life, death, and Resurrection (Mt 19:10–30). A moment's reflection makes clear that each of these three renunciations creates a vast void which empties a person of what the worldly world yearns for and pursues with unabated vehemence. It makes no sense to embrace the celibacy void without embracing at the same time the material goods void. Luke makes a point of linking the two renunciations once again when he speaks of those who leave all for the kingdom (Lk 18:29–30). Paul explains that the reason a virgin is a virgin of the Lord is that she focuses on the Lord with undivided attention. She is not a worldly woman (1 Cor 7:32–35). Celibate Paul rejoices to possess nothing (2 Cor 6:10). The most compelling connection between perfect chastity and poverty is seen in the person of Jesus himself. If we had nothing else, we have in him a powerful reason for seeing that the two ideals have an intrinsic relationship.

Secondly, Vatican Council II relates celibacy with factual frugality. Every time the Council fathers dealt with a celibate group in the Church, they counseled or required evangelical poverty of the members of that group. Bishops are told to give an example of "simplicity of life" (CD no. 15). Bishops and priests alike are invited to voluntary poverty, are to give to the poor or to the Church anything superfluous they may have, are invited to share in common, and are to have dwellings such that the poor are not afraid to visit them (PO no. 17). Religious are not only invited to be frugal; they are plainly told to be "poor in fact and in spirit" (PC no. 13). The bearers of the teaching office, therefore, see some inner connection between celibacy and poverty.

Thirdly, history through twenty centuries bears eloquent witness to this relationship. Through the ages religious orders have flourished when they observed evangelical poverty, and they declined when they became wealthy. As Raymond Hostie has shown in his study on the life and death of religious orders, many institutes eventually slip into a decline such that they finally disappear. Contemporary history tells the same tale: orders that live frugally are succeeding, while those that indulge in extensive wardrobes and expensive dining, drinking, and recreating are dying on the vine right before our eyes. This constant correlation between vowed celibacy and vowed poverty indicates an intrinsic connection.

Our fourth evidence is the expectations of the faithful, indeed, of those outside the Church as well. The laity commonly criticize religious and priests for lacking poverty. A woman who left the convent told me after a few months, "Father, you have no idea how much the laity criticize priests and religious for lack of poverty. When I was a sister, I heard nothing of it, but now that I am out in the world how much I hear!" Another was bitter when she spoke of her pastor, who constantly asked for money from the pulpit to run the school and yet himself went to Florida for his annual vacation. My point at the moment is not whether this criticism is justified or not. The point is that people see a connection between dedicated celibacy on the one hand and frugality on the other. They so commonly expect the two to be found together that we may infer that this *sensus fidelium* is itself an evidence of the connection.

Lastly, the very natures of the two counsels demand their being found together. There is something ill about a person who makes a surrender of the great human good of married love and then fixes his heart on mere things. Or to put the same idea a bit differently, it is abnormal to give up a dearly loved human person and then attach one's heart to subpersons. A healthy man or woman gives up married love only because he has found another and greater love. A religious head over heels in love with God does not fix attention on things. The normal celibate gives "undivided attention to the Lord" (1 Cor 7:35).

2. *Freedom from compensation compromises.* One of the sure signs that a person understands in more than a notional manner the celibate vocation is that he is free from corner cutting and from more or less subtle backtracking on sacrifices already embraced in principle. In the virginal vocation one gives up a human intimacy in exchange for a special divine intimacy. To surrender the one and then turn around and lose the other makes no sense. For the celibate to fix his attention on things is so abnormal the mere mention is proof enough.

By their vow of poverty religious choose to be factually poor and dependent in their use of material creation. Their motivation should be all that we have already described in Part Two of this volume together with what we shall note in the next section. If a religious is genuinely celibate (a condition that cannot be separated from right motivation), he is a man in love. Now a person who is in love cares proportionately little about things. The deeper the immersion in the beloved, the less is there concern about subpersonal reality. Consequently, a sister, brother, priest who travels extensively for pleasure, drinks and dines elegantly, spends a great deal of time and money on amusements, keeps a closet full of clothes, retains and enjoys superfluities is a person who is failing not only in evangelical poverty but in celibacy as well.

3. *The ecclesial dimension of the vow.* The Church herself is a poor pilgrim. All of us in every vocation are strangers and nomads on the face of our earth (Heb 11:13–16; 1 Pet 2:11). We entered this world with nothing, and we shall leave it with nothing. The conclusion: we should be content with necessities (1 Tim 6:7–8). Religious are people who are meant to live this pilgrim condition in a stark manner, a manner not required of all the faithful. They choose to leave their property for the kingdom, to surrender to a common fund the gifts they receive and the money they earn, to use money and material things sparingly and in dependence on the will of the community, a will articulated in the constitutions and applied by a superior.

We may recall that Scripture commentators are agreed that most by far of the New Testament texts on poverty are said for everyone in the ecclesial community. Some go further and hold that even Mark 10:17–22, Luke 18:18–23, and Matthew 19:16–22 are directed to all vocations in life. I find this last view unpersuasive both in itself and because it runs counter to the patristic understanding as well as to that of other contemporary exegetes. The Church herself has never understood that all men are invited or commanded to abandon their property for the kingdom. Religious are so invited, and they therefore live in drastic manners the life of the Church herself as a poor pilgrim. They are to be the cutting edge, showing by radical example that we have here no lasting city, that creation is meant to be shared, that an apostle is far freer when he is poor, that a detached person is much happier than a clinger. Just as the virgin lives in a literal and even a dramatic manner the bridal virginity of the Church (2 Cor 11:2), so the poor religious lives the pilgrim nature of the Church, plodding and suffering and yearning for the parousia.[1]

4. Has the religious vow changed in its meaning? In recent years popularizers and others in their private conversations have repeatedly said that the vow of poverty no longer means what it meant forty and seventy years ago. Whereas in the past this vow referred to a dependent and sparing use of material goods, it now is said to refer to using creation responsibly and to being available to others in one's time, talent, and person. Is this so?

At the outset I may make clear that the question is not whether responsibility and availability are desirable traits. They obviously are. The question is whether they are what the religious, canonical vow of poverty refers to. Several observations may be made.

First of all, no one can change the meaning of a vow once it is made. If ten years after I make a vow I change my mind as to what I wish it to mean, I am still bound to what as a matter of fact the vow meant ten years ago. No one unilaterally changes the character of a vowed obligation. The only respectable course of action open to me is to get a dispensation from my obligation and then assume a new one. This is why people who wish to change substantially the meaning of religious vows must leave their institute with a dispensation. Then they may, if they wish, form a new community

---

[1] *The Church Community*, pp. 40–42.

with a new set of obligations. If their new understandings are authentic, they may obtain canonical approval and standing.

Secondly, the sole conceivable authority capable of redefining canonical vows is the hierarchical element in the Church. And there is no evidence at all that any one of the three vows has been redefined either in Vatican Council II or in any other subsequent ecclesial document. I have found no serious theologian even try to support the above definitions of poverty. Popularizers and some retreat masters no doubt make statements like these, and unwary listeners have given them credence. Confusion and pain have unfortunately followed, but the reality of the vow remains.

Lastly, even the Holy See or an ecumenical council cannot change the revealed meaning of an evangelical counsel. By definition it is Gospel, Christic. No one can change the significance of the divine word. When the New Testament speaks of poverty as an ideal, it does not mean simply a responsible use of creation (everyone, even the married, are bound to this) or personal availability to others (all are bound to this too). Poverty in the New Testament deals with a sparing-sharing lifestyle, a way of life that promotes apostolic credibility and offers the world a pilgrim witness.

5. *The common life.* Twice in the Acts of the Apostles Saint Luke describes the ideal local church. It clings to the apostolic teaching, is devoted to community closeness, to the Eucharist, and to prayer (Acts 2:42). It likewise shares its material goods in common, so that members freely sell what they own and share the proceeds with all the others and according to the needs of each (Acts 2:44–46; 4:32–35). This remarkable use of possessions stems from a remarkable love: they have one heart and one soul (Acts 4:32). This radical sharing is so unusual that it is found almost nowhere in the secular world.

Scripture commentators often express the view that what Luke describes is the ideal Church, not what is obligatory upon the faithful generally. Max Delespesse faults these writers for failing to locate their exegesis in the traditional catechesis of the early Church, which taught the same as Acts. If we consult the patristic literature, we find that our ancestors in the faith looked upon this sharing at least as advisory if not as obligatory. In any event, in their living of the common life, religious attempt to concretize the ideal in a vowed community. They choose to give over to a general fund what they earn and receive as gifts on the one hand and to have their needs cared for from the same fund on the other. This, of course, is easy enough to say, but only detached people will do it in fact. We all have something of the squirrel in us, and until we are stripped of all selfishness we want to keep at least something of our gifts, if not our salary, and we want some of our needs and desires to be met by family and friends—especially when the community is unwilling or unable to care for them. And our human talent for rationalization reaches awesome proportions in our justifications of monetary desires.

We may trace out here in a concise manner a few of the implications of Gospel communality to which religious are committed in their profession.

The common life is rooted in love. In the New Testament outlook people so love one another that they wish their material goods to be possessed and used by these others as by themselves. Things we use as human beings are as extensions of our persons. The typewriter I am presently using is a continuation of my being insofar as it enables me, a thinking individual, to communicate my thoughts to others. This book in your hands is a continuation of your being as one who also thinks and wishes to share these same thoughts. Biblical writers suppose that because we love one another with a new love, we sincerely want others to share our good things.

It follows next that people freely choose this common life. It is not imposed but selected. There is no external force in taking religious vows. If I am rightly motivated, I want my brothers to share my gifts and everything I earn in speaking and writing. They likewise wish me to share in their gifts and contributions. We desire to turn in money received; urging or checking up should not be necessary.

Permission seeking, granting, denying are not red tape, not mere legal formalisms. I am perfectly willing to admit that only too often in the past and perhaps still at times in the present permissions have been legalistic formalities sought and granted so that "I do not break my vow." This is good, but it is not enough. The permission idea is based on the fact that what I use does not belong to me as an individual. It belongs to the community. When I use what belongs to the community, I must depend on the communal will, a will that must be articulated by someone who speaks in the communal name.

Because this person (leader, superior) is articulating the community's will, not his own ideas or whims, it further follows that he grants or denies the permission according to what the group has decided in its basic documents. While there must be room for discretionary power in the superior's judgment of particular situations, permissions ought not to be granted or denied according to the private opinions, strict or lax, of the superior.

Money in a religious order belongs neither to the superior nor to the individual religious. When it is used, therefore, the use should reflect the founder's mind and the chapter's concretization of that mind. General chapters should expect from the administration an honest accounting of how com-

munal resources have been handled. Likewise, major superiors should receive the same honest accounting from local
personnel. Superiors are stewards, not proprietors.

Monetary gifts ordinarily should be turned in to the common fund without an accompanying request to use the money.
A gift is not a reason for a religious to spend money. Need is
the reason. And needs should be cared for by the community whether one has a gift or not. If by way of exception a
gift is with permission immediately used by the recipient, it
may be used only if it does not belong to the individual who
received it. Religious have by vow given up ownership of
salary and gifts. Once a gift belongs to the community, all
have equal access to it.

What we have just considered applies likewise to travel.
Religious may not take trips simply because family or friends
are able and willing to pay for them. They who think otherwise bear the burden of showing why travel is an exception
to what we have already said. I have seen no one seriously
try to give a reasonable justification rooted in principles. If
in principle a trip may be financed outside the community,
there seems to be no reason why a person may not appeal to
private sources to finance his wardrobe, car, amusements, vacations, drinking, and dining. Then of course there is no
common life at all.

6. *Why is there so much inertia in practice?* In the past two
decades books, articles, reports, and position papers on religious poverty have literally poured out of printing presses
and photocopiers. I have spoken on the subject dozens of
times to sizeable groups, and others also have spoken. Yet
most of us will admit that with a few notable exceptions
(almost always in new foundations) very little change has
taken place in the living of the vow. A few individuals
have changed, some radically. But little has happened in

communities as such. Indeed, in many cases there is far less frugality than there was forty years ago. Why?

A good question. Is there malice or—what comes to the same thing—a deliberate unconcern for what the Gospel so plainly teaches? I should hope not. Is there a lack of information as to how this Gospel is to be concretized? In some cases, yes, but for the most part the answer probably should be negative. Has there been a confused proclamation? Yes, no doubt. And this is a major reason for the present book. Yet how many sincerely try to get their questions answered? People who want to be straightened out in other areas of human life normally seek light and advice. Confusion is a partial but not a full explanation for the inertia.

So we must ask again, why? Communal inertia is often due to the fact that upon discussing the implications of gospel ideals we tend to decide in the last analysis on a least common denominator. Men tend to disagree as to what "our poverty requires of us here and now", and so to preserve peace and not impose on anyone unwilling we settle for little or no change. The simple fact is that there are religious who can listen to the whole Gospel and still be unwilling to change their lives in any significant manner. Lest they be disturbed, the community decides on mediocrity—though, of course, it does not use that name.

A suggestion may be in order. I personally would not try to force someone to a level of frugality which he is not willing to embrace. Yet at the same time I would insist that this person ought not to be allowed to torpedo by his word or attitude what the rest of the group want to do in living the radical Gospel message.

There is yet a still deeper reason for communal inertia: we love our comfort, and frugality is uncomfortable. We are unwilling to give up unneeded pleasures, amusements, prestige, ease. Poverty demands suffering, self-denial, the paschal mystery. If anyone doubts that this reason is operative in his life, either he is a saint or he is blind. I would suggest that anyone who doubts it would do well to explore the matter in silent prayer before the Blessed Sacrament.

Religious Saints

Just as the married saints invariably live Gospel frugality according to the circumstances of their vocation, so do those who have taken upon themselves the evangelical counsels. Examples of this statement fill libraries. We may content ourselves with a few illustrations of the thoughts presented in this chapter.

Religious saints understood their vow of poverty as far more than "availability" or "responsible use". Saint Anthony's reaction to Jesus' invitation, "go, sell what you have, give to the poor and follow me" was to do exactly that. He disposed of his possessions and went into a life of solitude, manual work, prayer, and reading. His diet was bread and water, and he never ate before sunset. Later Anthony added a few dates to his meal, and in old age a little oil.[2] For Saint Benedict "a monk's life should always be lenten in its character", even though he did "not seek to impose a lenten observance all the year around".[3] Saint Dominic, reports Blessed Jordan of Saxony in his *Libellus*, "as a true friend of poverty, wore shabby clothes. In food as in drink, he observed the strictest moderation by avoiding delicacies and being content with simple fare." Saint Leonard of Port

---

[2] Butler, *Lives of the Saints*, 1:104–9.
[3] Justin McCann, O.S.B., *Saint Benedict* (New York: Doubleday Image edition), p. 135.

Maurice established a retreat house for religious and ordained for it a strict silence and a fasting diet of bread, vegetables, and fruit.[4] To the objection that a nun can be detached from what she possesses, Saint Alphonsus de Liguori answered that "whether you have an attachment to it or not, the possession of what is not necessary will always prevent you from attaining the perfection of poverty."[5]

Because they were not wedded to comfort and ease, the saints furnish no examples of inertia. In his life of Saint Francis of Assisi Thomas of Celano speaks often of the saint's poverty. One instance:

> All his sons and brothers lived in this same place with their blessed father, working much, lacking everything; very often they were entirely deprived of the comfort of bread, and they were content with turnips, which they begged here and there over the plain of Assisi. That place was so very cramped that they could hardly sit down or rest in it. But no murmur was heard over these things, no complaint.[6]

When Saint Dominic saw a house of his friars in Bologna being built in an elegant fashion, he simply put a stop to the construction work.[7] Though Saint Lawrence of Brindisi was the vicar general of his order, he slept on a straw pallet like all his confreres, and he washed dishes with them in the friary kitchen.[8]

Our first concern in this chapter was to point out the inner connection between virginity/celibacy and factual poverty. Saint Thomas Aquinas taught that they who intended

---

[4] Butler, 4:430.
[5] *The True Spouse of Jesus Christ*, c. 9, no. 2.
[6] *St. Francis of Assisi*, c. 16, no. 42.
[7] Butler, 3:263.
[8] Arturo da Carmignano, *St. Lawrence of Brindisi*, p. 77.

to live virginal chastity had also to live abstemiously and austerely with fasts and vigils.[9] Saint Vincent de Paul tied fidelity to poverty to fidelity to the whole of the religious commitment. Said he, "A Daughter who handles money is in very great danger of losing her vocation if she is not scrupulously careful that not a single halfpenny stays in her pocket for her own use." [10] If this strikes one as an exaggerated statement, he might reflect on the Gospel remark about fidelity to little things (Mt 25:14f.). No doubt diverse factors contribute to the "loss" of a religious vocation. Lack of poverty is not found in isolation—there will also be a lack of a serious prayer life. Yet it is unusually true that the eroding process begins with petty corner cutting and small infractions and unnoticed infidelities.

Authenticity succeeds. We have noted that religious orders that live this counsel tend to flourish, whereas those that do not tend to decay and disappear. Saint Pachomius, the founder of Christian monasticism, lived a life so austere that many would call it excessive (though he did not impose his rigor on others), but there is no successful argument against the results he achieved. By the time of his death in 348 Pachomius had 3,000 monks in his nine monasteries.[11] Saint Dominic experienced the same results; his order spread so rapidly that by the time of his death in 1221 the Dominicans counted over sixty friaries. Yes, authenticity succeeds.

[9] Martin Grabmann, *The Interior Life of St. Thomas Aquinas*, p. 60.
[10] Jacques Delarue, *The Holiness of Vincent de Paul*, p. 97.
[11] Butler, 2:259–62.

14

Clerical Poverty

There are two places in the New Testament where some of the listeners to Jesus and Paul greeted their doctrinal teaching with derisive laughter. On one occasion Paul had spoken of the resurrection of the dead to the men of Athens, and some in the group responded to his teaching with laughter (Acts 17:32). On the other occasion Jesus had spoken on the right use of money when "the Pharisees, who loved money, heard all this and laughed at him" (Lk 16:14). It may be significant that in both of these cases of the closed mind the subject under discussion was of a bodily, material reality.

It may also be significant that among the subjects that most readily incite opposition in clerical and religious circles, both liberal and conservative, are those that deal with material reality: comfort, clothing, pleasure, traveling, drinking, and dining. As long as a speaker or writer remains sufficiently abstract, as long as he does not infringe upon tangible reality, he can be as radical as he likes. But as soon as his remarks threaten a comfortable way of life, he invites rejection. Few of those who live comfortably are willing to listen sympathetically to the serious suggestion that they ought to dine and dress and recreate less elegantly. We speak willingly and readily about the poor in Bangladesh or India or Africa, but we are not so willing to eat simply, possess a sparing wardrobe, eliminate much of our pleasure traveling and upper-middle-class recreations. The human heart has not changed much in twenty centuries.

Yet Jesus' response to this closeminded rejection of his teaching about frugal living was anything but mild. He responded to the Pharisees' derision with a scathing denunciation of their hateful external appearances covering over an absence of inner goodness: "You are the very ones", he retorted, "who pass yourselves off as virtuous in people's sight, but God knows your hearts. For what is thought highly of by men is loathsome in the sight of God" (Lk 16:15).

Yet one does not have to be particularly perceptive to realize that the well-off ambassador of Christ presents a pathetic picture. Anyone who reads the New Testament knows that Jesus both lived and taught a factual frugality, that his consuming concern was the Father and his will, that he cared nothing for material comfort and abundance. Pathetic must be the word, therefore, to describe the herald of this poor Christ, who lives a life of which the Master would have no part. This herald is pathetic also because people generally tend not to take him as seriously as he would like to suppose. If we wonder why twelve men transformed an empire when thousands of us seem to transform so little, the reason is not hard to find. The sainted bishops and priests we shall mention further on were widely admired in their spheres of influence because their lives fit their message. They were taken seriously even by those who had not the least intention of imitating their way of life. Whatever else people might think of them, they do not think of them as saying one thing and living another.

Despite all this and the importance of it, the witness value of pastoral frugality is not its deepest reason. An ecclesial leader is by definition a radical man. He is so burningly athirst for the kingdom that he cannot be bothered with fine food and stylish clothing. He is a singlehearted radical who yearns for the Lord day and night (Is 26:8–9), who has put his hand to the plow and does not turn back. He with Paul minds the things of heaven, not those of earth (Col 3:1–2), and he untiringly pursues the presence of the Lord (Ps 105:4). Unashamedly he refuses to dilute the message of the Gospel (2 Cor 4:2), and he loves his brother even to death (Jn 13:1). He is a man who literally leaves everything, yes, everything for the reign of the Father (Lk 18:29–30), and while he has nothing, he possesses everything (2 Cor 6:10).

The Gospel leader is a person in love. And people in love are unconcerned about things irrelevant to their love. Jesus was blunt on the point. He said that it is pagans who are concerned about their lives, about what they eat and drink, what they wear (Mt 6:31–34). They who pursue the kingdom are to be so singleminded that they scarcely think of food, clothing, housing. Even less does it occur to them to be concerned about luxurious drinking and dining, about recreations indulged in by the upper classes. They would be ashamed to be seen on expensive vacations or with extensive wardrobes.

The main reason for apostolic frugality is a positive absorption, a being in love that makes the pursuit of worldly goods appear both ludicrous and useless. Just as a man and a woman in love with each other see reality in a whole new light, so people in love with God see themselves, others, and things in an entirely new perspective. Saint Paul tells us that the worldly person cannot understand what the Gospel says about things of the Spirit (1 Cor 2:14). He cannot therefore understand the contents of this volume. To him it is nonsense. Barring a conversion, no homily, no admonition, no book is going to change his mind.

This positive absorption, this being in love with God is perhaps the chief reason why a frugal way of life lends credibility to pastoral work. Modern men are weary of weavers of words, people who say beautiful things but do not live them. They are looking for authenticity, for heralds who have met God in deepening prayer and can speak of him from their hearts. They are looking for leaders who have met their Lord in personal encounter and can speak of him from their own experience.

If we wonder how our thousands of clergy produce so little impact on the masses, no little part of the explanation can be found here. Almost no one thinks of bishops, priests, ministers as poor in fact. There are some happy exceptions, but for the most part we appear to people as very much interested in upper-middle-class living. It is difficult for them to be much affected when we talk about the scriptural themes of sacrifice, detachment, self-denial, renouncing superfluities, carrying the daily cross, dying with Christ to this world. If they found us at prayer as often and as long as they find us before television sets or on golf courses or in elegant restaurants, they might take our homilies more seriously. We all know why people flocked in astonishing numbers to the confessional of the Curé of Ars.

Seminars and articles on pastoral approaches and methods can be useful. They are needed. But without radical witness, they are sterile. Times are different, yes, but it is not beside the point to remark that twelve men transformed an empire without a single course on methods.

To her brother, a parish priest, Saint Margaret Mary Alacoque wrote:

> It is absolutely necessary to eliminate three things. The first, attachment to earthly things, especially the love of pleasure. Gambling is included in this. The second, everything superfluous in your dress and in your personal habits. What you save in this way you must give to the poor. Thirdly, be as

little mixed up in the things of the world as you can, not allowing yourself any wilful self-indulgence.[1]

Saint Claude de la Colombière received for his office at court, preacher of the Duchess of York, a pension far beyond his needs. He therefore took a vow to devote the surplus money entirely to the poor, to good works, and to supporting converts to the faith.[2] Saint Francis Borgia as Duke of Gandia and Viceroy of Catelonia was originally a great one in the world's eyes. Later as a priest he was not above begging food or wheeling a barrow of manure or sweeping a floor or digging a hole or doing menial tasks in the kitchen.[3] Saint Vincent de Paul believed that the clergy should work hard and earn their bread. Said he, "we live on the patrimony of Jesus Christ by the sweat of the poor. On our way to the refectory we should always think, 'Have I earned the food I am about to eat?'"[4] Saint John Vianney's deliberate poverty is so well known that we need recall no illustrations of it here. But we may not forget that the official Church has expressed her mind about sacerdotal frugality in designating the Curé patron of her parish clergy.

Contrary to what many people would expect, examples of voluntary episcopal poverty abound. When he became a bishop, Saint Francis de Sales imposed upon himself a rule of life which included stipulations bearing on frugality. He was not to wear silken robes, and yet his clothes were to be "clean and suitably made". He renounced the episcopal fineries apparently common in his day: scented gloves, silk muffs, sashes,

[1] *Letters of St. Margaret Mary Alacoque*, translated by Clarence A. Herbst, p. 94.
[2] Georges Guitton, *Perfect Friend*, p. 297.
[3] Margaret Yeo, *The Greatest of the Borgias*, pp. 157–58, 165.
[4] Jacques Delarue, *The Holiness of Vincent de Paul*, pp. 96–97.

stockings, shoelaces, extra rings, and furs. The food offered to his guests was to be "frugal and yet at the same time clean and properly served".[5]

Once he was appointed cardinal, indeed, forced against his vigorous and persistent resistance, Robert Bellarmine was given by Pope Clement "four sets of robes, purple and scarlet, which was three more, the recipient said, than the Gospel allowed. Of these he took such care that they lasted till his death, twenty-two years afterwards, the cuffs only having been renewed when the old ones were past all patching."[6] The cardinal lived on bread and garlic, and he denied himself a fire throughout the chilly Roman wintertime.

Though he also was a bishop, Saint Thomas of Villanova mended his own religious habit in order to save a little money for the poor.[7] Saint Antoninus gave his money, furniture, and clothes to the poor.[8] Saint Charles Borromeo, a cardinal, wore shabby clothes and avoided all personal elegance. We are told that his servants "had to use many artifices to make him put on new clothes".[9]

Saintly successors of Peter have lived in this same manner. Saint Pius X, for example, wrote in his will, "I was born poor, I have lived poor and I wish to die poor."[10] Millions of us witnessed on television the wordless but eloquent homily on poverty given by Pope Paul VI lying in a small pine box during his funeral Mass in huge Saint Peter's Square. Later his personal secretary, Monsignor Pasquale Macchi, revealed that the Pontiff often wore sackcloth under his

---

[5] M. V. Woodgate, *Saint Francis de Sales*, pp. 59–60.
[6] James Brodrick, *Robert Bellarmine*, pp. 157–58.
[7] Butler, *Lives of the Saints*, 3:614–15.
[8] Ibid., 2:263–64.
[9] Cesare Orsenigo, *Life of St. Charles Borromeo*, p. 325.
[10] Butler, 3:477.

vestments during liturgical ceremonies. "Many of those who watched the opening of ceremonies of the 1975 Holy Year . . . had compassion for the exhaustion with which the Pope walked. No one could possibly have imagined that in addition to his chronic arthritis his sides were covered by the rough sackcloth, some of which penetrated his flesh." The Pontiff had worn sackcloth from his youth.[11]

Though all this is plain and in the public record, we still find some clergymen who resist the notion that they are to live simple, frugal lives. Where they get their principles is for them to say, but in any event they explicitly reject as meant for them what saints commonly do. What we do hear proclaimed sometimes is moderation in the use of material goods, their own concept of moderation. They think that the Church herself proposed nothing more as ideal for priests and bishops. This view deserves some attention, for even if it is not often proposed in published form, it is frequently lived in actual life.

What is in the Church's mind? It is not correct to say that she merely counsels moderation. In the *Decree on Priestly Life*, no. 17, Vatican Council II states that after bishops and priests care for their decent livelihood and the fulfillment of their duties of state, they should devote what money remains "to the good of the Church or to works of charity". That is more than moderation. Furthermore, says the Council, "they are invited to embrace voluntary poverty. By it they will be more clearly likened to Christ and will become more devoted to the sacred ministry." That is far more than moderation. Yet more follows: "Priests as well as bishops will avoid *all* those things which can offend the poor *in any way*" (italics added). The popular *Constitution on the Church in the Modern World* was still more demanding. Twice, in nos. 69 and 88, the faithful are told to give

---

[11] *National Catholic Register*, Oct. 7, 1979, p. 2.

to the poor from their "substance" and not merely from superfluity. None of this is mere moderation.

Preparation for the priesthood, said Pope Paul VI, requires "a *demanding* asceticism" which, however, is not suffocating. A priest must practice "self-denial in the highest degree", for it is an essential condition for following Christ. Celibacy is connected with personal asceticism. Priestly life, says the Holy Father, "requires a truly virile asceticism both interior *and exterior.*" [12] Once again we are beyond a mere moderation.

It is sometimes objected that we should not take too seriously the radicality of New Testament texts on poverty because, after all, Jesus did go to banquets. His priests, therefore, need not worry if their dining and drinking surpass the measure of ordinary lay folk.

This objection is so superficial I am tempted to delete it from our discussion, but since there are people who think this way, a few words of reply may be useful. Of course the Lord attended banquets—what frugally minded priest even today can avoid all of them? Courtesy often requires attendance. It says nothing about one's own free choices. Further, it is interesting to notice what Jesus said at one of the meals he did attend, for it demolishes the notion that one ought to treat himself elegantly in food and drink. "When you give a lunch or a dinner, do not ask your friends, brothers, relations, or rich neighbors, for fear they repay your courtesy by inviting you in return. No; when you have a party, invite the poor, the crippled, the lame, the blind" (Lk 14:12–14). When people eat and drink well, whom do they usually invite? For another indicator of what Jesus thought about this dining-well question one may consult Luke 16:19–31.

---

[12] *Sacerdotalis caelibatus,* no. 70, 79, italics added.

PART V

JOY

15

Happy Are You Poor

Poverty is not popular. Though we gratefully live in the midst of a biblical renewal, it would be a mistake to conclude that therefore everything in Scripture must be widely acceptable among Christians. It would be no problem at all to list a dozen themes that both are prominent in the New Testament and are rarely spoken of from most pulpits. Among these we may mention self-denial, temptation, sin, evil or idle talk, sparing-sharing way of life, virginity, detachment, continual prayer, hell, heaven. Factual poverty is one of these unpopular subjects.

It is popular to speak about the third and fourth worlds and to assail the injustices of nations, but this sort of oration leaves both the speaker and the listeners in their comfortable modes of life. Hence no one much objects. It is fashionable in religious circles to speak and write about joy and celebration and resurrection, and for this there are many ready ears. But it is quite another matter when it comes to penance, mortification, sorrow, suffering and asceticism. There are no best sellers that deal with these subjects.

Factual poverty is so unpopular that many of those who make a public profession of it have in recent years redefined it to suit their tastes. This we have noted in Chapter 13. Rather than have it mean what the Gospel says it means, namely, a materially sparing life, it is now said to be a "respectful use of creation" or a "sharing of one's time, person, and talent". These new definitions are convenient, for they exact next to nothing.

This unpopularity should not surprise us. We ought not to imagine that saints invariably lived their thoroughgoing poverty in welcoming circumstances. As a young priest Saint Louis de Montfort was assigned to a community that was "like a country club for privileged priests and seminarians.... They wore silks and satins ... gaudy velvet jackets.... Few wore the prescribed clerical garments. Few said Mass.... Nobody preached." [1] Yet there can be little doubt that these men had their euphemisms to describe what they were doing, and their euphemisms were probably not unlike the current ones: "We must be relevant ... our hard work requires these amusements and this sort of drinking and dining ... one must dress according to his milieu ... we ought not to be different from others ... we have a right to culture and travel ... the rich, too, have to be saved."

Factual poverty freely embraced can easily enough trigger opposition in one's own family. Both Saint Stanislaus Kostka and Saint Albert the Great aroused the ire of their fathers when they entered upon the poor manner of life of the early Jesuits and Dominicans, respectively. The former was abused in a paternal letter for putting on "contemptible dress and following a profession unworthy of his birth", while the latter was subjected to the rumor that he might be removed by force from his religious house. [2] Human nature does not change much.

Popular or not, frugality in faith brings joy. Indeed, in the words of the Lord himself, it is a blessed condition (Lk 6:20).

[1] Eddie Doherty, *Wisdom's Fool*, p. 90.
[2] Butler, *Lives of the Saints*, 4:336, 345.

His teaching would rank at the bottom of the opinion polls, but unmistakably it is his teaching nonetheless.

The Cynic's Outrage

"Happy are you poor." By all standards of this world these four words are intolerably false. They seem to be an insult to the billions of human beings at this moment enduring the slow, grinding torture of empty stomachs, cold nights, crawling vermin, lingering insecurity, gnawing idleness, premature death. The cynic on hearing this beatitude will offer his sneering response: "You who say this can never have been destitute. In your warm comfort you have never rubbed elbows with the really poor or darkened the doorways of their hovels. You have not shared their rodent-infested rooms or experienced their marginal who-cares-about-us existence. You are a great one to talk about the happiness of being poor. You are romanticizing tragedy. This moralizing soothes your guilty conscience. Happy are the poor. . . . Indeed!"

The cynic's response appears plausible, but its first flaw should be obvious. It fails to recognize that neither you nor I originated this beatitude. We are too dull to utter a thought so brilliant. He who spoke it did know poverty from the inside. He was born in dire circumstances, and he died with absolutely nothing. In between times he chose to have no place to lay his head. He loved the poor, and he gravitated toward them. He was one of them. He was romanticizing nothing.

The second flaw flows from a failure to make a distinction between destitution and frugality. It is true that those who lack nourishment, shelter, and clothing often live a lingering despair. Rarely do we find a sparkling smile on their passive and prematurely wrinkled faces. But Jesus did not favor or promote destitution. Rather he demanded that his disciples do all they can to rub it out by feeding the hungry, clothing the naked, visiting the ill and the imprisoned. Precisely because he did require a most liberal sharing of possessions did he promote personal frugality. Yet for all these qualifications we may not dilute the Master's beatitude. Even the destitute, if they are loving persons, are in far happier circumstances than the tightfisted rich. "Woe to you rich ones; you have your consolation now" (Lk 6:24) is also part of the divine judgment. If the poor are of goodwill, if they avoid an eroding bitterness, they are far more open to the Gospel message, to the ultimate values of human life. They are far less subject both to petty and to gross attachments, to the blinding results of numberless clingings, to a callous indifference to the needs of others. Because they have no treasure here below, they are more likely to seek the ones that are above.

Our cynic's final mistake is superficiality. He views the linking of poverty and happiness as ridiculous because he does not think. He reflects the unreasoned feelings of the world. He assumes that happiness and sense comfort and pleasure are all one and the same reality. Because in his view pleasure equals happiness and because comfort and pleasure demand money, the poor could not be happy. They have nothing with which to buy this desired condition.

What Is Joy?

That we may avoid these mistakes we are thinking together in these pages, even though this does take some time and a modicum of effort. Our initial inquiry at this point bears on the differences between sense pleasure and human joy. While many people take them to be synonymous, we shall notice that they differ in several important ways. Once we see these differences, we shall be prepared to understand both what Jesus means by his beatitude and why he is right.

The reader should note that we are distinguishing sense pleasure from joy. Intellectual or spiritual pleasures (perhaps better called delights) are closely akin to joy, even though they may not be in every way identical. What then are the main differences between sense pleasures and human joy?

Pleasures are localized in a particular part of the body. Delicious food delights taste buds but nothing else. Joy is not restricted to one bodily area; rather it accompanies a general well-being of the person as a person. It is compatible with bodily suffering.

Pleasures are caused by a specific material stimulus: food, drink, fragrance, color, sexual contact. Joy arises either from intellectually appreciated stimuli (beautiful music or scenery) or from immaterial reality itself (a brilliant idea, superb literature, moral goodness, authentic being in love). Pleasure springs from things, for it is a surface phenomenon. Joy springs from beauty and goodness; it is deep in origin and cause and effect.

Pleasures are severely limited in duration. Not only do they last only for a given length of time, but if one makes an attempt to extend them unduly, they issue in satiety and disgust. Too much ice cream at one time leads not only to eventual illness; it can lead to a dislike at the moment itself. Joy on the other hand tends to perdure, and the deeper it is the longer it lasts. The deepest joy lasts forever: "Rejoice in the Lord always" (Phil 4:4). It begins on earth and lives through eternity. It never leads to satiety or to disgust. One cannot experience too much truth or love or beauty. And of course joy never leads to illness. On the contrary, the more joy, the greater is one's health as a person.

Because mere pleasure depends for its very existence on material things, it can be taken away either by a more powerful adversary or by the sheer exhaustion of excessive experience. Because joy does not derive primarily from visible creation, it can suffer from neither robbery nor depletion: "I will see you again, and you will be filled with joy, and that joy no one will take from you" (Jn 16:22).

Though they are good in themselves, sense pleasures tend so to capture the heart of fallen men that they easily lead to excess and evil. Peach pie is good, but it readily leads me to a second or third piece and thus to intemperance, with all the unfortunate consequences for psychological, bodily, and spiritual health. Pleasure tends to lead a person to fix his desires and center himself in this finite realm. Joy, on the contrary, leads one to good. It expands one's horizons and inclines him to the origin of all joy. It liberates the human gaze and focuses our sight on the infinite. Joy opens to heaven.

Yes, the authentic poor are happy, and the clinging wealthy are not. They who abound in material goods are stimulated for short periods of time, but the stimulation soon leads to satiety, boredom, consequent emptiness, and sometimes disgust. These experiences entail no sense of overall well-being. One can feel miserable in the midst of plenty. There is often the accompanying fear that one's property will be harmed, stolen, or lost on the stock market. Because this person places his security on earth, his spirit is always in prison. It may be a splendid prison, but it never permits him to soar to the glories for which the human heart has been made. He knows next to nothing about joy. In fact, he thinks pleasure is joy, and no one can convince him otherwise. He does not understand that his wealth holds him captive. Only a regenerating word can liberate him. If he would make the Lord's word his own, he would have the truth, and the truth would set him free (Jn 8:31–32).

The Theory Works in Practice

Plain honesty requires that we assert that the New Testament teaches an unblushing and uncompromising asceticism, a hard road and narrow gate, a carrying of the cross every day, a renouncing of all that one possesses, a being rid of superfluities, and a dying with the Lord (Mt 7:13–14; Lk 9:23; 14:33; 1 Tim 6:7–8; Rom 6:3–5). But it also teaches a rich, abundant human living, a complete and intense joy beyond understanding, a joy no one can take away, a rejoicing in the Lord always, a tasting of the very goodness of uncreated Beauty (Jn 10:10; 15:11; 16:22; 1 Pet 1:8; 2:3; Phil 4:4).

To the worldling the idea of finding joy in frugality is absurd, for to him joy is nothing more nor less than sense pleasures. He knows nothing deeper, nothing more lofty. And sense pleasures can be unceasingly multiplied only with money, abundant money, the more the better. But deep down, though he kicks the heels of his spirit in a refusal to face it, the worldling does know that sense pleasures bring happiness to no one. He knows that something is radically missing in his own life. The cartoons in his slick magazines show that he knows that the wealthy are bored to death in the dullness of their cocktail parties. There is a sprinkle of pleasure here and there, and it is *de rigueur* to put on a brave front and a superficial smile, even though one feels the gnawing emptiness aching in his heart.

The worldling will not face his colossal inner blah. He multiplies experiences in an unending and desperate attempt to numb his spirit. It hurts so much not to have attained the very reason for his existence, an immersion in God, that he uses things as a narcotic. The worldling pursues prestige or comfort or wealth or sexual encounters not because they basically satisfy him (if they did, once would be enough) but because they dull his inner aching. Always and eventually he is faced with his personal failure. But the sight of it is so revolting and painful, he dives once again into the aspirin sea of frantic pursuits.

The saints know better. Having tasted the best, they know how to assess the least. Having drunk at the Fountain, they spend little time with the trickles. They know both from the word of the Lord and from their own experiences of it that indeed the poor are happy. Saint Paul can speak of super-abounding in joy in all his sacrifices and tribulations. It is this apostle who reports to us the remarkable example of the Macedonian churches, which joined a constant cheerfulness to their intense poverty, and from this extreme neediness they begged for the favor of sharing what little they had with another church (2 Cor 8:2–4). If one looks upon a sparing-sharing way of life as dismal, dull, forbidding, his imagination has conjured up a nongospel picture. Buddhist asceticism may be smileless, but the Christic cross begets delight.

Saint Augustine is a prize example of the point I am making. Only those persons can compare pleasures competently who have had experience of them. This is why the world-ling's testimony is of so little value. He knows nothing of what transcends the senses and the natural intellect. Intel-lectual genius that he was, Augustine knew the keen delights of the mind: music, literature, art, nature, philosophy. Sinner that he likewise was, he also knew the pleasures of the flesh from his years of living with a woman to whom he was not married. Later as a converted mystic, he knew the delights of advanced prayer. His *Confessions* is a classic account of where happiness is to be found and where not. For him God is his entire delight:

"O my Father," he prays, "supremely good, beauty of all things beautiful . . . O Truth, Truth, how intimately did even the very marrow of my mind sigh for you . . . I hungered for you. . . . You are my God, and I sigh for you day and night. . . . Sending down your beams most powerfully upon me, I trembled with love and awe."[3]

This man is now taken in a love that renders pale his former love: "What cries did I send up to you when reading those psalms! How was I set on fire for you by them, and how did I burn to repeat them. . . . I have tasted you, and I hunger and thirst after you. You have touched me, and I have burned for your peace."[4] So superior is Augustine's new delight that its normal completion could be nothing less than heaven: "Sometimes you admit me in my innermost being into a most extraordinary affection, mounting within me to an indescribable sweetness. If this is perfected in me, it will be something, I know not what, that will not belong to this life."[5]

No one has a right to contest Augustine's account of the relative merits of human delights unless he has himself experienced all that the saint experienced. In other words, only the mystic may discuss the matter intelligently. Any other is like the man born blind who denies there is any such thing as prisms and rainbows.

One who knows the saints well knows also that their habitual state even in the keenest suffering and deprivation was a state of joy, a deep inner delight in God. Those who have read widely in the lives of these heroes and heroines need no

[3] Book 3, c. 6; bk. 7, c. 10; trans. John K. Ryan (New York: Doubleday Image edition), pp. 83 and 171.
[4] Book 9, c. 4; bk. 10, c. 27; pp. 210, 255.
[5] Book 10, c. 40; p. 272.

example of this truth, but for those who have no considerable acquaintance with them a few illustrations may be of use. Saint Catherine of Siena is surely one of our race's most glorious women. I shall not narrate her feats of action and contemplation (she was a marvel in both), but we may not fail to remark that this austere, lovely virgin was the recipient of literally unspeakable experiences of God. She could say of herself that "my mind is so full of joy and happiness that I am amazed my soul stays in my body. . . . And at the same time so much love of my fellowmen has blazed up in me that I could face death for them cheerfully and with great joy in my heart." [6]

Among the many traits for which Saint Thomas More is famous is his penchant for being "merry". No sooner was he committed to the Tower in anticipation of a grim death than he wrote to his beloved daughter, Meg: "Our Lord be thanked, I am in good health of body and in quiet of mind: and of worldly things I no more desire than I have. I beseech Him make you all merry in the hope of heaven. . . . Written with a cole (probably a piece of charcoal) by your tender loving father." [7] Before he was arrested, Thomas had seen the handwriting on the wall. He gave up the chancellorship and its revenue and calmly faced the coming poverty with his family: "Then may we yet, with bags and wallets, go a-begging together and hoping that for pity some good folk will give us their charity, at every man's door to sing *Salve Regina*, and so still keep company and be merry together." [8] One would be hard put to find in one sentence flowing from real life a better, more attractive conjoining of poverty and joy.

[6] Raymond of Capua, *The Life of St. Catherine of Siena*, pt. 2, c. 6; p. 167.
[7] E. E. Reynolds, *St. Thomas More*, p. 245.
[8] Ibid., p. 209.

Saint Francis of Assisi is so well known as an example of the delight attendant on gospel poverty we need not cite him. Less known is Saint Philip Neri. Elsewhere in this book we have noted his asceticism and poverty. Here I should like to recall his vivacious personal charm, his inexhaustibly warm affection, his burning love for God, and his ecstacy at prayer. He may also be called the laughing, joking saint. Visiting Philip, his contemporaries agreed, was a delight. His younger followers said of him that "Philip's room is not a room but a paradise".[9] Saint Alphonsus de Liguori proposes Saint Mary Magdalene de' Pazzi as an example, for when this saint had no bread at the table she was so happy at her deprivation that she later "accused herself (to the abbess) of having entertained too much pleasure" in it.[10]

There is little doubt that the man of the world is inclined to reject all this as pious puff not worthy of serious consideration. He is dreadfully superficial but is unaware of it. He is so out of touch with his deep self and his inner aching void that he has no idea of the grossness of his mind. He needs prayer more than argument, for he cannot understand the things of the Spirit (1 Cor 2:14).

Nonetheless an invitation to reflection is in order. John Henry Newman has commented on the deep delight found in an inner aloneness free of the clutter of things:

> The Christian has a deep, silent, hidden peace, which the world sees not, —like some well in a retired and shady place, difficult of access. He is the greater part of his time by himself and when he is in solitude, that is his real state. What he is when left to himself and to his God, that is his true life.

---

[9] Theodore Maynard, *Mystic in Motley: The Life of St. Philip Neri* (Milwaukee: Bruce Publishing, 1946), p. 158.

[10] *The True Spouse of Jesus Christ*, chap. 9, no. 2.

He can bear himself; he can (as it were) joy in himself; for it
is the grace of God within him, it is the presence of the
Eternal Comforter, in which he joys. He can bear, he finds
it pleasant, to be with himself at all times, —"never less alone
than when alone." He can lay his head on his pillow at night,
and own in God's sight, with overflowing heart, that he wants
nothing, —that he "is full and abounds," — that God has
been all things to him.[11]

Why Is It So?

Now we must ask why frugality embraced in faith brings
joy. Few people would consider the answer obvious. To see
clearly we must delve deeply. Down in the inner recesses of
the human spirit there is a center that opens on to infinity.
We basically hunger not for things but for everything. We
thirst not for drips and dabs but for the originating fountain.
Our deepest hungers are not for food and drink, not for
amusements and recreations, not for property and wardrobes, not for notoriety and gossip. We hunger for truth, we
thirst to drink beauty, we yearn to celebrate, we seek to delight, we stretch out to love and to be loved. That is why
anything less than everything is not enough.

Property, wealth, diversions, amusements are often obstacles to the attainment of truth, beauty, celebration, delight,
and love. They are not evil in themselves, of course, but the
fact is that they allure us to fasten on them for themselves.
They become finite crutches that distract and lead us away
from our genuine quenching. Pulled to them, we cannot be
pulled to God. We cannot serve God and mammon. The

[11] *Parochial and Plain Sermons*, vol. 5, sermon 5 (San Francisco: Ignatius Press,
1997), p. 1003.

choice is either/or, not both/and, and we have the divine word for it—as well as human experience. It is not accidental that people with money typically amuse themselves with an endless series of loveless experiences. It may be elegant dining and drinking. It may be endless hours of vapid television. It may be one sexual encounter after another. It may be the vain living in other peoples' mind through a slavish concern for "what they think of me". It may be pride in possessions or education or background or social standing.

To the extent that things are important to a person, love diminishes. Men and women in love scarcely give a thought to things. When they are not in love, there is not much else that they think about but things. Even other people become things to them.

Happy are the poor because they suffer no thing impediments to what they most deeply crave. They are free to rejoice in the Lord always. Such is at least part of the reason why one cannot be a disciple of Jesus unless he renounces *all* that he possesses (Lk 14:33). When this complete surrender occurs, one is then able to experience a fullness of joy, not just a trickle of it: "These things I have said to you, that my joy may be in you and your joy may be complete" (Jn 15:11).

What we are saying bears intrinsic connection to the transforming union of prayer development. One has only to read the *Confessions* of Augustine or the *Spiritual Canticle* of John of the Cross or the *Interior Castle* of Teresa of Avila to know well that there is no delight on the face of the earth to compare with that found at the summit of prayer growth. Even before one reaches this loftiest stage, he may grow so far as to experience the absorption of ecstatic prayer. He finds there a joy so enveloping, so captivating, so piercing that his sense contact with the outside world is suspended for a time. There is so much delight within that the without fades away. It is this to which gospel living normally leads. Vatican Council II speaks of the faithful, lay as well as religious, growing in their understanding of divine revelation through their contemplation of divine realities and their experience of them (DV no. 8). The same faithful are spoken of as experiencing the paschal mysteries *fully* and burning with love during the liturgical celebrations (SC no. 10). Apostolic religious are presumed to possess *fully* the treasures of mysticism (AG no. 18). Priests, all priests, are likewise presumed to live and work from an "abundance of contemplation" (LG no. 41).

Poverty of fact and of spirit contributes to the radical self-emptying that is a condition for this fullness of prayer and joy: "Having nothing, possessing all things" (2 Cor 6:10). God forces himself on no one. If I cling to things, he lets me have my things. If I am empty of things, he fills me with himself. Paul can assure us that our eyes have not seen and our ears have not heard—indeed, we cannot even imagine—what God has in store for those who love him (1 Cor 2:9). The poor are indeed happy. They have Everything.

16

An Examen

This book does not have as one of its purposes the tracing out of a finely worked out frugality blueprint indicating to each reader exactly how he must live its message in practical details. The Church's function is to proclaim the Gospel, not to solve all of life's specific problems. Once the Gospel is proclaimed, each of us has the task of applying it to his own situation in all the intricacies of a concrete life.

I entertain the hope that the main outlines of the New Testament message on the use of material creation have been presented with neither exaggeration nor dilution. Since many of us find it difficult to apply ideals to a life situation, I have thought that an examen might be of some help in focusing our thoughts on practical solutions. The questions that follow are best pondered in a prayerful context.

Attitudes

Am I thoroughly convinced that the Gospel message on the use of material goods is directed to *me*?

Have I sincerely tried to understand without rationalization what this evangelical poverty means?

Does the Gospel affect me, change me? How different am I today from what I was one year ago?

Am I a person who latches onto ideas simply because I like them and not because I have sought and thought through the evidences for them? Have I done this regarding popular notions of poverty? Am I doing it in other areas?

Am I willing to embrace the self-denial and suffering gospel poverty necessarily entails?

Have I actually lived as though I could serve God and mammon?

Problems and Presuppositions

Am I in love with God? If not, why not? What else matters?

Am I total in pursuing him? If not, why?

Do I consider myself a stranger, a nomad, a pilgrim on earth? Or do I find myself very much at home?

Am I living a serious prayer life? Am I growing in prayer depth? Do I expect to understand poverty and to live it without a deepening prayer life?

Am I something of a relativist, that is, do I tend to consider contradictory opinions as equally valid or equally invalid? Have I thought through this matter as it is treated in Chapter 3?

Do I take positions and cling to them even when I have not studied their pros and cons?

Do I see how my sinfulness and my sympathies color what I hold in religious and moral matters?

Am I humble enough to accept the doctrinal messages of Scripture and the teaching of the Church Jesus himself established to speak in his name? Or do I assume I have an access to the Holy Spirit that is denied to Jesus' representatives?

Could I explain to an inquirer why evangelical poverty is not dirt or disorder . . . or destitution . . . or miserliness . . . or mere availability . . . or insensitivity to beauty?

Have I read sufficiently well-documented lives of the saints that I may know how they typically think and act, how they heroically concretize the Gospel? Where honestly is my center of gravity? Of what do I like to speak when I have a willing listener? Do I give Gospel poverty a bad name by personal slovenliness or laziness or by a sour disposition?

Values of Gospel Poverty

Do I understand what radical readiness for the kingdom means? Could I explain it to another? Do I experience anything of this readiness, this sensitivity? Do I need to review Chapter 6?

How do I stand regarding the world's basic values: prestige . . . comfort and pleasure . . . sexual excitement . . . success . . . money?

Do I rationalize my lack of factual frugality on the plea that "after all, I am detached from what I have"? How can I prove to myself that I am detached, poor in spirit?

Do I tend to equate my level of to be with my level of to have . . . my worth with my possessions?

Am I happy when at times circumstances require me to go without a necessity?

In my zeal to be poor have I turned poverty into an end sought for itself rather than for what it makes possible? When would I be making poverty an end in itself?

Am I vividly aware that sharing with the needy is a condition for possessing a living faith (Jas 2:14–17) and therefore of being in the state of grace (1 Jn 3:17–18)?

Is my concern for the dire destitution of the millions in the third and fourth worlds mostly abstract, or does it change my concrete manner of living? Do I so live that I/we have something to share with them?

In what ways have I shared with the world's forsaken ones in the last twelve months? Do I view the poor with reverence and loving compassion? Should I/we give our Christmas and birthday gifts to the needy rather than to friends and relatives who often do not need what they receive?

Do I/we give to the poor not only from our superfluities but also from our own need?

Is my way of life so different from that of the unbeliever that my compatriots know well that my homeland is not here below (Heb 11:13–16)?

Does my care for exterior adornment betray where my heart actually is?

Do I in my person enhance the Gospel's credibility? Are people brought closer to God through their contact with me? Are they attracted to what is good, beautiful, and noble (Phil 4:8–9)?

As an apostolic person have I pondered Jesus' austere teaching on missionary poverty? (See Chapter 8.) Am I making sincere efforts to live this teaching?

Does my lack of impact on the people I serve have any discernible connection with what they see in me . . . and do not see?

In my daily round of activities do I really look on myself as a stranger and pilgrim here on earth? Does the thought of heaven influence my choice of food, clothing, recreation, television?

Do I place my security in things rather than in God? Do a higher salary, a paid-up mortgage, an insurance policy lull me into thinking that "now I am all set"?

Does my pilgrim status prompt me to want only necessities? Am I a hoarder? Do I save superfluous things?

Have I practically embraced the consumerist philosophy of "the good life"? Do I consider myself as called to witness against this philosophy by a sparing-sharing manner of life?

The Married

Have we in our marriage worked out a balance between caring for the family on the one hand and for the poor on the other?

Are we in vain in our dress . . . our home . . . its furnishings . . . our car . . . our other possessions?

How are we to apply in our married life the Gospel's sharing doctrine?

Am I person centered or thing centered?

Do I understand how questions in other sections of this examen apply to me?

Religious

Do I see that my celibate dedication requires that I be poor? Do I want both celibacy and poverty? Do I see that it is abnormal for a religious not to desire both counsels?

Do I live as a witness to the pilgrim Church? Am I sensitive to the fact that others view me as representing the Church?

Do I desire the common life, or do I simply tolerate it? Do I want to turn in salaries and gifts and keep expenses to a minimum? Do I avoid outside private sources for money, clothing, travel?

Have I contributed to community inertia by my own mediocrity? By my love of ease, comfort, pleasure?

Am I content with simple fare at the table? Do I travel more than I need to? Does my closet look like a poor person's closet?

Would saints feel comfortable in my recreations and vacations?

Am I glad to do menial tasks around the house?

Are generous young people attracted by the unusual character of my way of life, or do they see me as indistinguishable from people who do not claim to follow Christ?

Clergy

Do I with Saint Paul mind the things of heaven, not the things on earth? Is my "meat to do the will of the Father"?

Does my style of life render credible what I say in the pulpit about sacrifice and self-denial?

Do people somehow get the impression that I am in love with God? Are they, for example, likely to speak to me about deep prayer, thinking that I would understand them and cast some light on their questions?

Am I as a priest practicing "self-denial in the highest degree" as Pope Paul VI said priests are to do?

Do the quality and depth of my prayer (priests are to "abound in contemplation" according to Vatican Council II, LG no. 41) lead me to desire gospel poverty?

Conclusions

Can people conclude from my manner of life that my center of gravity is not in this world? Does my use of creation speak God to them?

Do I expect that one who lives evangelical poverty will be criticized by those who do not? Do I accept this criticism amiably and with a cheerful disposition?

Am I sensitive to the fact that my deepest hunger is not for things but for Everything? Does this realization govern my day-by-day choices and decisions?

INDEX